I0641237

CONTENTS

Front cover: "Denizens of Dystopia" by **Kathrine Savu** (acrylic on canvas, 2020) • Interior drawings ("Silly Little Guys") by **Nadia Arioli** • Photograph ("Radial") by **Bradley David**

© 2024 Sagging Meniscus Press
All Rights Reserved

ISBN: 978-1-952386-97-8

exactingclam.com

Exacting Clam is a quarterly publication from Sagging Meniscus.

Contributing Editors: Jake Goldsmith, Tomoé Hill, Kurt Luchs, Melissa McCarthy, M.J. Nicholls, Thomas Walton
Contributing Metaclamician: Christopher Boucher
Senior Editors: Jeff Chon, Elizabeth Cooperman, Tyler C. Gore, Doug Nufer
Fiction Editor: Charles Holdefer • *Poetry Editor:* Aaron Anstett • *Reviews Editor:* Jesi Bender
Executive Editor: Guillermo Stitch
Publisher: Jacob Smullyan

You're Dropping Out, There, Houston

*

An ellipse is a shape; plural, ellipses. It's the surface that's exposed when you set a cone point-up on a table, then cut through it while tilting your sword somewhat from the horizontal. It's an oval, a closed loop, where for every spot on the curve and for any pair of focal points within, the sum of the two distances from the perimeter to the two points remains the same.

Ellipsis is a form of punctuation; plural, ellipses. It conveys, in English, omission. Other languages use the same typography—three dots in a row—for a wide range of subtly different meanings. Conversely, other alphabets, eg Laotian, use a different symbol (like a shepherd's crook) for the same concept, of leaving out some words.

But here in written English the three dots are used to show that the speaker said something more, but the writer is not going to report it all fully. Or, perhaps the speaker hesitated a little, or they trailed off, whether because they didn't want to finish, or couldn't, or because they were implying an opposite. It might be that . . .

Sometimes as a writer you use ellipsis when you can't quite be sure what the words were. There were sounds, but you could not swear, not with enough certainty, what they said. Indeterminate or imprecise reporting. In email, ellipsis is used in a little three-dot image, showing that the reply has been trimmed, that more, prior conversation is stowed below, out of the way. For a symbol depicting omission, ellipsis certainly contains a lot, still.

**

I've been considering—or perhaps looping around while staying at a constant combined distance from—two particular literary texts, which contain several of these modes and uses of ellipsis. The first text is, *Composite Air-to-Ground and Onboard Voice Tape Transcription of the GT-4 Mission*, published by NASA, Manned Spacecraft Centre, Houston, Texas, August 31st 1965. Aka *NASA Program Gemini Working Paper No. 5035*. It was declassified in 1974, and is available online, as a scanned pdf of the doc. I'll be referring to it as "the transcript," and it's fantastic.

GT-4 means that it's the Gemini-Titan programme, fourth mission into space. What's that? Blasting off on 3rd June 1965, two astronauts, Ed White and Jim McDivitt, spent ninety-eight hours in orbit, carrying out various experiments such as testing camera equipment, monitoring their own physiology, looking for the South Atlantic Anomaly. They tried, unsuccessfully, to align their craft with their discarded booster. And Ed White had the particular task of being only the second person ever to undertake an EVA, or, Extravehicular Activity: he walked out into space.

The transcript records most of the radio conversation between the space craft and the various stations back on earth (on land and ships); they communicated with whichever one was closest, losing contact with others as they went round and round, sixty-six times. Like with friends—sometimes you talk to one more, then another, then you come back into range with the first.

***

There are two astronauts on board, Jim the command pilot and Ed the pilot. My sense from reading the transcript as a text, a script, is that Ed is by far the more personable and relaxed of the two. He gives a somewhat "awestruck stoner" vibe, in contrast to Jim's practical, military demeanour. Did you remember to turn off the magnetometer and the proton-electron measurer, Ed? "I'm afraid I was watching the stars so much I forgot to turn it off at the proper time," is his comment at thirteen hours, three minutes, thirty seconds after the start of the journey. I do know that this, my interpretation, can't be factually true, because I don't think one becomes a NASA experimental pilot without a large complement of sensible, obedient efficiency. But that's how it reads, when you take the transcript as a literary text, when you interpret it. For example, at around six hours forty-one, Jim is giving ground control a long debriefing about the booster: "All the ΔV [delta velocity] I'd added up to that time had been in the direction of the booster, or retrograde. [. . .] it seemed like our rates on the booster were low, on the order of a half a degree a second in pitch and yaw. [. . .]

(I'm using square brackets and three dots, the ellipsis, to indicate that there are some other words in the transcript here, but I'm not including them because they distract from the main thrust; I don't have space in my vehicle. The typist of the transcript itself uses five dots to indicate ellipsis, instead of three. Just a cultural habit. Let's resume . . .)

"On the other hand, I wanted to make sure we had a reasonably good alinement prior to getting to our 2-1 GO-NO GO point in case anything went wrong," says Jim, still going on about his retrograding. At this point Ed distracts him with some chewing gum. Jim continues the tech chat, about acceleratometer bias, camera access, vehicle separation, until he's interrupted by Ed blissing out: "Boy! That was beautiful. [. . .] That first view of the booster. [. . .] Just exactly." While not floridly articulate, Ed really manages to convey his sense of awe and pleasure. And he's funny.

Not everything is recorded here; the transcript omits their broadcasts that went out live to the public on earth. The transcript also doesn't explain *what* they're talking about, which is fine, makes it more immersive to read. Some of it is just exchange of numbers, tech details that they have to agree on. Sometimes they say regular, comprehensible words, but there are gaps. It seems that they're talking at cross-purposes, or the transcriber can hear some utterance, but it is too indistinct to write down, to pass on to us. E.g. here's a snippet of conversation from twenty-six hours five minutes:

Jim: It looks like a rain storm with rain hanging out except that it's . . . . .
Ed: How about yawing a couple . . . . .
Jim: . . . . . the other way?
Ed: . . . . .
Jim: . . . . .
Ed: How far around do we have to come yet?
Jim: Can you see it?
Ed: What?
Jim: . . . . . parallel.
Ed: . . . . . to come around to the side?
Jim: Yes.
Ed: . . . . .
Jim: . . . . .
Ed: Those are the lights we saw the other night.
Jim: Was it like that, Ed?
Ed: Huh?
Jim: It wasn't like that.
Ed: . . . . . horizon.
Jim: . . . . . California.

Sometimes the text is entertainingly truncated: there's a mysterious exchange, or creative cut-up, at thirty-five hours seventeen where we aren't told Jim's words, but Ed's are:

"Right. I just finished it. /
. . . . . sunrise /
That thing really grabs me when it goes like that. /
Have you got a good view of it out there? /
. . . . . get to sleep . . . . . /
Yes. /
Ah . . . . . cereal."

Some information has not been preserved, here. Also, it's a scanned page, and some of the typing doesn't show up enough on the pdf. It's too faint, the distinctness of the words fading into the white of the page. Occasional typos.

Then there's a crucial exchange, at thirty-six hours four minutes:

Jim: Sure wish I knew how our water supply was doing back there.
Ed: I do too.
Jim: . . . . .
Jim: . . . . .
Ed: I don't think so. Do you?
Ed: . . . . .
Jim: . . . . .
Ed: Why don't you see if you can see, Jim?
Ed: That's really neat!
Ed: Nothing. Absolutely nothing.
Ed: Maybe you can direct it better.
Jim: . . . . .
Jim: . . . . .
Ed: No way of telling, huh?

Degree zero, void, no content. I don't know what they're talking about here. No way of telling, huh. I mean, from what I know about the context of what they're doing on the mission, I know it's something about taking photos, and trying to align the horizon and the rising stars, and use the equipment right, while intaking enough water so they don't dehydrate but not so much that they run out. But it's beautifully vague. Surrounded by ellipses, out in nowhere, there's a particular and precise absence and omission, which Ed nonetheless manages to articulate: "Nothing, absolutely nothing."

* * * *

Ed's comment on seeing and nothingness is, for me, the highlight of the expedition. But there is another excellent section of the transcript, and in fairness this is the part for which the journey is mainly famous. It's Ed leaving the capsule after four hours of elapsed journey, going out on his space walk. He has a much better time of it than his Russian precursor, who got steamed up, too hot. Ed enjoys his EVA ("This is the greatest experience I've . . . . . it's just tremendous.") In fact, he enjoys it so much that they cannot get him to come back into the vehicle. His feet went out at four hours thirty, though the reader senses that the spacewalk really starts at four eighteen, when they finally manage to open the stuck mechanism on the hatch door and Ed looks out properly for the first time, "What a view! By golly. You can see the black sky up above."

During the EVA there's a bit of a comms problem, with Jim inside his space craft having to relay everything between ground and Ed. At four hours thirty-six they inform Ed, "You've got about five minutes." He doesn't come in, and they allow another five. But he won't come in even after this extension, despite them shouting "Get back in!" at him, not til four hours forty-eight minutes. And then it goes terribly quiet. From the space end; from earth there's a constant request for, "Gemini 4, Houston CAP COM. Gemini 4, Houston CAP COM. Give me your status." But they don't. At five hours fourteen we read Ed and Jim chatting to each other. It's not until five nineteen that they report directly back to earth.

This thirty minutes of drop-out, non-communication, a pause or lacuna in the two-way radio conversation during and after Ed's space walk, is great. It seems that they were having trouble with the door mechanism again, and decided to concentrate on this, as having a hatch that closes as you re-enter earth's atmosphere is more pressing than talking to Gus down in command. But I think, I prefer to read the text as, that they undergo this quiet time because Ed has experienced something so extraordinary that he cannot yet convey it in words. He's moved out into an unexamined space, come to a new understanding of his position vis-a-vis the capsule, the other humans, the earth, the source of light. He looks different, and differently, now.

He's lost for words. Or, some words are lost. Most of them, they left Ed's mouth, travelled all the way to ground control, landed in their ears, on the magnetic tape, and on the page. But not all of them. Where do the other words go, then, the ones from the ellipsis? They disappear, dissipate, fade out somewhere between Ed in space and the transcript in my hands. There is a long distance, through a cold, harsh environment, and there are a lot of stages, over which the information could decay. But I think that it's in space that we lose his words. If they haven't reached us, they must still be floating about out there, out in orbit, words like the sparks from the booster rocket that Ed describes as spreading out into his field of vision like stars, or like "little fireflies all around." It's very beautiful, the picture of space he conveys with his words.

Ed White: born, 14th November 1930, died 27th January 1967—less than two years after his space walk—in another rocket, the Apollo 1. He was in the cabin, still on earth, when a fire broke out, killing the three astronauts on board.

✳✳✳✳✳

This lapse in communication between unusual vehicles—I've seen that before somewhere. In Hergé's *Cigars of the Pharaoh* (original serialisation in French, 1932-34; book, 1955; English translation, 1971), which is my second focal point, here. Quite early on in the story, Tintin, Snowy, and their new friend, Sophocles Sarcophagus, wake up one morning floating in the Red Sea, each in his own coffin. They've been tossed overboard in a hurry when the coastguard approached the boat they were on. Tintin in a coffin in a boat was jettisoned. Soon he will be swamped by a tribute to Hokusai's *Wave*, and picked up again by a gun-runner, while Sarcophagus is spiked with the poison of madness. It's all go, in Tintin.

But on this one page, the three coffins, looking like they're roped shut but luckily they're not, these coffins float together on the dark green water, until dawn. When they wake up and push open the lids, Tintin and Snowy are right next to each other, so they can chat. But Sarcophagus is further away, and when he talks, Tintin can't hear him. Sarcophagus says: ". . . ry . . . cet . . . ing . . . wo . . . ump . . . ca . . ." (That's in English. In French, he says, ". . . té . . . oua . . . our . . . pa . . . ote . . . ère . . .") Tintin retorts, "What? What are

you saying? . . . Louder. The noise of the wind is drowning your words." Sarcophagus replies to this complaint, "What? I can't understand a word you're saying with the wind." Because all he can hear from Tintin is ". . . ous . . . al . . . ent . . ."

There's a third frame of cartoon, where the same thing happens: they only receive fragments of what the other is shouting. Sarcophagus is on a distant horizon by this point, waving his arms as though he's semaphoring, and six little pips, spots of water, sparks, radiate around his head like the hour marks on a clock. So Tintin gives it up, realises there's no point in shouting himself hoarse, and he's better off attaching his boat to Snowy's and trying to fish them some breakfast.

Now, this is an excellent page in the Tintin oeuvre. Both participants in the conversation that we see parts of the two ends of are saying and demonstrating the same thing, which is, I can't hear you say that you can't hear me. What do the ellipses mean in this situation? That some sound is carrying, over the waves, through this channel, but not enough for Tintin to distinguish the precise words. The noise of the wind drowns out the specificity; only fragments get through. And where are Tintin's words going? Parallel to Ed's words falling away into space, Tintin's words, because of his environment, his circumstances, are clearly falling into the sea (just ask his friends Thompson and Thomson). That's where they'd drop: into the water.

In both these cases, the transcript and the cartoon, we're presented with, there's a definite focus on, the ellipsis. The voice drops out, we're left with absence. This then invites the question of, what flows in to fill the space? It might be silence. Absolutely nothing. Or static, or buzz. Sibilance, or indistinct noise, or imagination. I think there's a clue in our typography, where the ellipsis is shown by three dots, because in Morse code (and there's a lot of this to decipher, in Tintin) these three dots have another meaning: they're the letter "S." That's what I hear rushing into the holes in the communications between the death-related vehicles: a long hissing sound. Sss tss tss in every ellipsis, everywhere.

******

We have floating around in space through the gaps and dots, and we have floating in coffins with ellipses. There's one further instance that grabs me, one voyage around these two focal points, the one in the water and the other up among the stars. It's in Chapter 110 of Herman Melville's 1851 *Moby-Dick,* when Queequeg notices that the Nantucketers have a habit of carving wooden vehicles (or, coffins,) for their dead sailors. He approves of this, as it's like what they do back at his island home: put the dead warrior in a canoe and float him away "to the starry archipelagoes; for not only do they believe that the stars are isles, but that far beyond all visible horizons, their own mild, uncontinented seas, interflow with the blue heavens; and so form the white breakers of the milky way."

(That's Queequeg who signs up to the voyage by copying a tattoo off his arm, the one in the shape of "a queer round figure"—an ellipse.) The ocean, with its strange vehicles, extends right on up into space, and death, believes Queequeg. I'd go along with that; it's easy to trace the continuity between Tintin's ocean, up to the Gemini's ellipsoid orbits through space. Just follow along the dotted line . . . There's one other thing that we might notice, though, linking the two spheres.

The astronauts are anxious not be left waiting in the water too long, after they splash down. They say it's because they don't want to drown, and they have been in this extreme, extremely confined space for a long time. But I wonder if it's something a little more, which is bothering them in the water. Queequeg certainly has a horror of being ignominiously dispatched into the sea without the right craft; he's scared of the "death-devouring sharks," as Melville calls them. And what does Tintin find, when, floating there in his coffin, he trails a spar overboard? He hooks . . . a massive shark which nearly capsizes and destroys him. That's what is dot-dot-dotted about him in the water, in his expanse, sea, space. They're all around, though we might omit to mention them. That's what lives in the ellipsis, or just under it, cruising all round us: s . . . s.

Kat Meads

The Second Wife's Tale

Twenty years before his first gubernatorial triumph, George Corley Wallace Jr. of Clio, Alabama, campaigned for the favor and affections of Lurleen Brigham Burns of Tuscaloosa, achieved his objective, proposed marriage and was accepted. He was 23; she was a just-graduated-from-high-school 16. The couple had met at a Kresge's dime store, where Lurleen worked the cosmetics counter. "He had the prettiest dark eyes, and the way he'd cut up!" a smitten Lurleen recalled. She was a Southern gal who preferred the outdoors and being in it, hunting, fishing, swimming. In appearance, she was "small and rather mousy . . . not an easy woman to spot in a crowd," according to journalist Shana Alexander. In a backhanded, narrow-field compliment, *Wallace* biographer Marshall Frady deemed her "attractive in that hard, plain, small-faced, somewhat masculine way that Deep Southern women tend to be attractive." She had zero interest in politics. But when her power-hungry spouse, unable to succeed himself as governor, had the bright idea of running her as his shadow puppet in 1966, Lurleen obliged, won the election and died in office, age 41, from cancer.

Restored as Alabama's governor, two weeks before his 1971 inauguration, George Wallace married another Alabamian, Cornelia Ellis Snively, 20 years his junior, divorced mother of two and niece of previous Alabama governor Big Jim Folsom. The eventual husband and wife first laid eyes on each other when a past-bedtime, nightgowned Cornelia, age seven or eight (depending on the source), was spotted spying on her uncle's party in progress from the grand staircase of the Governor's Mansion by the Wallaces. In Cornelia's telling, Lurleen declared

Cornelia a "mighty pretty little girl." "And I'll bet you'll be even prettier when you grow up," George added (according to Cornelia).

None described the second Mrs. Wallace as mousy. In *Settin' the Woods on Fire*, a PBS documentary on the life and political career of George Wallace, commentator Wayne Greenhaw extolled "knockout" Cornelia's raven-haired beauty and ability to "fill out a pair of blue jeans." Cornelia's mother, Big Ruby, never one to hold back with the press, expanded on her daughter's physical attributes: "All us Folsoms got big tits." The Folsoms, men and women, were a tall bunch; George Wallace leveled off at an unimpressive five feet, seven inches. "Not even titty high," Big Ruby dismissed.

Lurleen Wallace had been a retiring, biddable spouse, a woman never entirely comfortable in the spotlight. With his marriage to Cornelia, Lurleen's widower joined forces with a different sort of partner. Neither retiring nor biddable (guided, perhaps, by maternal example), the second Mrs. Wallace had lived in and loved the spotlight since her childhood residence in the Governor's Mansion when Big Ruby had served as her widowed brother's official hostess. By dent of family ties and legacy, Cornelia had occupied the Governor's Mansion when George was a mere governor wannabe—not a fact Cornelia was inclined to ignore or downplay in life or in her memoir. "I came from a political family a mile long," she informs us, the uninformed, in *C'nelia*. First Lady Frances Folsom Cleveland, wife of U.S. President Grover Cleveland, was a distant relative. When "Uncle Jimmy made his first bid for the United States Congress, Mother campaigned for him the entire nine months she carried me . . . I absorbed my political instincts while in my mother's womb," Cornelia writes. Politics, "the king of sports," is her raison d'être: "I was born in it, I lived in it all my life and I've loved every minute of it."

In 1973, on assignment for *Newsweek*, Shana Alexander journeyed to Alabama to jointly interview the Wallaces. By the end of that chat, Alexander had concluded that Cornelia Ellis Snively Wallace was "the best thing that could possibly have happened" to politico George.

Judging by her memoir, Cornelia heartily agreed.

The title of her book is the spelling of her name as it is "correctly" pronounced "in the South," the "*r* silent," Cornelia explains. It is also a signal that George Wallace, while present and accounted for, will grace the pages in relation to *her*, which is not to say the author is unaware her story is being read in no small part because of her connection to *him*. Shrewdly, she begins with the day of the shooting, the most known and public "event" of the Wallaces' lives together: "May 15, 1972: To say that it began like any Monday morning at the Mansion would not be true." Her husband, sights now set on the U.S. presidency, was "unusually irritable, agitated and fidgety." He wanted to cancel, doubting that "one more day of campaigning could change the outcome of the primary elections" in either Michigan or Maryland. But there was always the chance that the newspaper and television coverage of those last-ditch efforts would keep Wallace's name at the forefront of "voters' minds" as they set off for the polling booths. And so the Wallaces set off for another day of campaigning.

One of the ways *C'nelia* aims to convince readers it possesses the virtue of accuracy is to provide an abundance of detail with regard to George Wallace's medical condition, surgeries, care and feeding from the moment Arthur Bremer pumped multiple bullets into the presidential candidate as he glad-handed supporters in the parking lot of a Laurel, Maryland shopping center . . .

(George) had a superficial wound on his right forearm and a superficial wound on his right upper arm . . . There was a flesh wound at shoulder level in front and a deep grazing wound above his right shoulder blade. One bullet had entered his stomach, traveled around and lodged in the left flank. Another entered between his sixth and seventh ribs and lodged in the spinal canal.

Reporting on the first paralysis tests, Cornelia quotes verbatim from the "medical charts" ("On the basis of slight denervation activity of diffuse distribution and encompassing the myotomes . . .") for two full pages. When infection sets in, Cornelia shares the details of "a bulge as large as a grapefruit" on her husband's side, which, lanced by the surgeon, "gushed . . . enough pus to fill a fruit jar."

In the aftermath of the shooting, Cornelia vows that George will "never see her cry," goes without food or sleep for the "first three crucial days," disdaining the help of "coffee," "tranquilizers" or "artificial props," deals with family, doctors, press and visitors (approving of Ethel Kennedy's athletic good looks, dissing Richard Nixon's "television makeup" atop "grayish" skin). When a secret service agent, prompted by Cornelia, shares what he has written about her in his report ("either the bravest woman you've ever met or a fool"), Cornelia assures the agent and her readers: "The lady is not a fool." Who is Cornelia Wallace? *C'nelia*'s cause and function is to convince us she is a glamorous, courageous, devoted, savvy, multi-talented, God-fearing, tough love-administering woman, standing by her man.

A slim book, *C'nelia* is plumped by photos of the Alabama Governor's Mansion "bought by my Uncle Jimmy." The Folsom clan entire. Cornelia, age four, in a "gypsy" Halloween costume. Cornelia, the striking debutante, in evening dress. A beguiling photo captioned "Me and my friend Martha Mitchell" that, disappointingly, has no textual counterpart of Cornelia and Martha swapping political gossip and advice. Many are the campaign photos: her uncle on the stump, her husband on the stump, Cornelia smiling and standing beside a standing George in the early going and smiling and standing beside George in a wheelchair after his paralysis. As readers will expect, there is a reproduction of the photograph first published in the May 26, 1972 edition of *Life* of a struck-down Wallace, Cornelia shielding his body from further attack with her own. Amid narrative particulars about the assassination attempt, Cornelia discusses hairdos. On that fateful day, a local hairdresser had styled Cornelia's hair: "I doubt that Ed could have done any better even if he had known . . . that hairdo would appear on the cover of *Life* magazine," Cornelia breezily surmises. Done with chronicling the challenges imposed by the assassination attempt on man and marriage—and how she rose to meet each and every one of those challenges in response—Cornelia turns to happier times: her idyllic existence as a coddled child within the Folsom family nest.

B orn in Elba, some 80 miles south of Montgomery, Cornelia flourished in a small town setting and recommends the same environment for all youngsters. ("Growing up in a small town is an experience every American child should have.") Her father, Charles Ellis, a civil engineer, did not, as time revealed, live up to Big Ruby's manliness bar. Whereas her mother was "gregarious, assertive and ambitious," her father was "conscientious, serious and inhibited," Cornelia writes. "No matter how hard he tried, Daddy could not outmeasure the Folsoms. Neither could any of his achievements match those of Jim Folsom, who was the yardstick by which my mother measured all men"—a yardstick her daughter clearly shares.

C'nelia tracks no downside to the parental divorce, only advantages. Raised thereafter with her brother in the Governor's Mansion alongside widower Big Jim's two youngest daughters, Cornelia assumed leadership of the children brigade, pampered and praised for her looks, talents and social grace. By age eight, she possessed her own stack of "calling cards." Young Cornelia played piano and saxophone, danced ("tap, bal-let and toe"), performed as a majorette and recited poems "at assembly." In high school, she wrote for the school newspaper, sang in the choir and served as church organist on Sunday nights, already a staunch, baptized Christian. All the stars aligned until they didn't. Flabbergasted by her early elimination in the Miss Alabama beauty contest, she swore "never again to enter the Miss Alabama contest." Other disappointments loomed. As a University of Alabama freshman in Fall 1957, she was "shocked and terribly crushed" to be "noticeably left out" when sorority rush "invitations were issued." The reason, according to Cornelia: her uncle's "liberal" politics. "People said Jim Folsom was too soft on the question of integration." Insulted because no one at the time "bothered to ask" whether she "shared" her uncle's opinion, in her memoir Cornelia clarifies: she was and is staunchly anti-integration. "Segregation now, segregation tomorrow, segregation forever!" would not be an issue that divided Cornelia and her future husband.

Snubbed by UA sororities, in a fit of pique, Cornelia transferred to Huntington College in Montgomery. Passing on campus accommodations, she boarded with mom. Living with mom, if mom was Big Ruby, put no damper on a daughter's ambitions and plans. Big Ruby pulled some strings, got Cornelia a screen test with MGM Studios in New York and drove her daughter to the big city during Christmas break. ("I wanted her to be a movie star all her life," Big Ruby later told the press.) Cornelia preferred to audition for MGM's record label. Since Cornelia's is a memoir more about politics than music, her MGM recording contract, songwriting (e.g., "Baby with the Barefoot Feet"), romance with Phil Everly, and touring years with Roy Acuff are logged rather than explored. A job as the featured water-skier at Cypress Garden in Florida brought with it "a new outlook on life. It was like getting paid while you were on a summer vacation." And then, with only locale serving as transitional link, a one-paragraph summary of marrying for the first time and becoming a mother: "While I was skiing at Cypress Gardens I met and married John Snively III" (described elsewhere as a "wealthy citrus grower"). "I had two sons, Jim and Josh Snively, before my marriage ended tragically in divorce seven years later, in 1969."

The stage was set for a return to Montgomery and a reconnect with Uncle Jim's one-time protégé George Wallace. Cornelia decided to attend a Wallace rally with her sons, she explains, because she "wanted them to appreciate their political heritage." (Appreciate their heritage or glimpse their future? the reader may reasonably wonder.) "Now that (Wallace) was virtually the most eligible man in town, I began to think of him in a different way," Cornelia writes. The courtship remained discreet, given Lurleen's recent passing. When Cornelia realized she'd "fallen in love with George," she "tried to analyze" her attraction. The reason she came up with: "In essence, he was every man I had ever loved all in one."

As presented by Cornelia, the every-man-in-one she loved was hard of hearing, requiring her "to pitch and project (her) voice in such a way" that her "words never fell on deaf ears." His favorite condiment was ketchup, which he poured liberally on most food placed before him. His favorite TV show was *Hee Haw*. "Like all good politicians, he was very conscious of 'bad breath.'" He "loved to read his mail." He "got very annoyed if members of the road crew laughed or talked loudly while his speech was in progress." As a politician, he was "cagey, crafty . . . the hero of countless political battles," beloved for his "gutsy, aggressive style." As husband and wife, "every morning" the Wallaces "enjoyed the intimacy of sharing the bath." Wallace liked to receive foot massages that Cornelia liked to administer. ("It was a private thing we shared and one from which he derived much pleasure.")

The twosome married with their "children's blessings" in 1971. They were still "enjoying the blissful ecstasy of an extended honeymoon"

when Wallace "embarked on the whirlwind presidential campaign of 1972," Cornelia writes, assigning a number to those days of bliss: "I was a bride of only one year and four months when my husband was suddenly gunned down in Laurel, Maryland on May 15, 1972."

In its final chapter, *C'nelia* returns to its author's uphill battle to "pump up" her depressed, disabled husband who wants only to stay in bed, indulge in crying jags, and call her "mama." (Cornelia nips that "mama" business in the bud.) She refuses to countenance the "self-pity" George is "drowning" in, reminds him that he has "had to struggle all his life" and will "triumph over this tragedy as he had the others." When that battery of encouragement fails, she plays the God card, as in: what happened happened because it was "part of God's plan."

At last comes the day when Wallace acknowledges Cornelia's predominant role in his two-year "complete recovery." In that "precious" moment, Cornelia writes, George "poured out his heart to me . . . told me how very much he loved me . . . that he couldn't have made it without me . . . how much he appreciated all I had done for him." In response, Cornelia "felt a deep and total contentment that only comes with the security of true love."

It was a security short lived. A year after Cornelia's memoir was published, the fractured state of the George/Cornelia union became widely known when the *Washington Post* reported that a "small blue van" had pulled up to the Governor's Mansion on September 6, 1977 and "moved out" Cornelia and her belongings. Away from the public eye, the marriage was in crisis . . . In *Wallace*, Marshall Frady furnishes a taste of the operatic drama and acrimony of the final split. Cronies whispered in George's ear about Cornelia's liaisons; she, in turn, tapped George's phone, convinced he was indulging in phone sex with "prior consorts." Initially, when trouble came calling, Cornelia dug in her heels, refusing to divorce. "George wanted the divorce. I didn't," she later told *People* magazine. "There were other people influencing him . . . People who wanted to be close to George's power fought to get me out of the picture." Each party sued the other. Ultimately, in an out-of-court settlement, Cornelia received $75,000 and a portion of the community property. But Cornelia wasn't done. Even after the divorce papers were signed, Frady reports, the former first lady would occasionally "storm" the mansion, only to be "forcibly ejected." She also stayed on in Montgomery. As had predecessor Lurleen, Cornelia ran for governor, joining a field of twelve other candidates in the 1978 race, one of those aspirants her Uncle Jimmy, 69 years old, "legally blind and partially deaf" (*Washington Post*). Unlike Lurleen, Cornelia did not triumph. In a statement to the press, she blamed her failure on the sitting governor, who had refused to endorse the candidacy of wife number two. When rumors began to swirl that George planned to marry again, a woman thirty years younger this time around, Cornelia "issued a public call for prayer by Alabama's citizens to avert that gruesome prospect." It was evident to any and all, Frady reports, that Cornelia was "wheeling into a full Folsom-scale breakdown." In 1985, her mother and brother had her committed to Searcy Hospital, a state-owned and -operated facility in Mount Vernon, Alabama. Upon release, she once again moved in with Big Ruby . . .

George Wallace died in 1998. As for Cornelia, cancer "killed her dead," as they say in the South, at the age of 69 in 2009. In one of her last interviews, she announced that she was working on a second book, a "political," "historical" novel, working title *The Giant Slayer*. The main character, she said, closely resembled her Uncle Jimmy. A second, less heroic character was based on ex-husband George, "who needs to slay the giant in order to feel big." There was also a character based on herself, a woman who "functioned very well at a high-paced fever pitch"; a woman who, when she "wanted something, kept going until she wore everybody down."

In *C'nelia*, tucked among reminiscences of her sublime childhood, Cornelia describes a happenstance sighting of Zelda Sayre Fitzgerald, strolling along a fashionable Montgomery street, alone. As a third-grader, Cornelia didn't realize her "eyes had fallen on a tragic romantic heroine," the "wife of a literary genius." As an adult memoirist, Cornelia doesn't seem to grasp she is describing her situational kin: another ambitious, frustrated, Alabamian woman unsatisfactorily married to a man more famous than herself.

Tomoé Hill

The Obsessions

'You take a picture then move on', the man says curtly in a German accent. I am paraphrasing from someone else's recollection, but it hardly matters; the point is that there is no moving on with obsession when you sense its presence. Conversely, those who cannot sense it do not understand why others linger in it. People abhor being alone, and it is so evident here in the exhibition. Even near paintings they move to crowd the spaces between, immediately in front of, yet the contradiction—the inherent dissatisfaction of humanity—lies in the fact that alongside that fear, they cannot remain with a thing, a person which immediately shows them their true selves. If they do not recognise themselves in the real, they sense it in the abstract, and if one cannot sit with the self in the shape they are, how could they possibly sit with the self which is there to reflect their unbearable nuances?

I count the precious seconds where there appears emptiness before the paintings. I cannot go further than four. Four seconds before the unbearable sense that to be alone must be conquered; four seconds is all the restless mind and eye can bear before it captures without seeing what it beholds.

It is the obsessives I have always had time for. The fuck-you-get-on-with-it types like Mark Rothko or Rainer Werner Fassbinder, where blood and paint or cinema or whatever the poison is is the same, where everything is too much and not enough, and more often than not—because obsession is like a car with no brakes—they do not stop as much as crash, in the end. It is not a glorification of that well-abused word, *genius*, as much as an acknowledgement that life is sometimes about one thing with not enough time, the horrible contradiction being in the time you cannot be fully about that one thing, time drags and sometimes you along with it. What presents as preventable cliché is also, occasionally, an unpreventable reality of the obsessed. When the terrible space is there, you fill it—it fills you—with depression and anxieties, drugs and alcohol, love or whatever most resembles it, or worst of all, nothing; all that a poor substitute for your one true thing.

Obsession is every colour in the world at once. The way they made us paint colour charts in art school so we would learn about complement and theory and it was enough to drive everyone slightly mad: crying at 2am over blends and tones and what went where—what *could* go where—and the sheer impossibility of calculating nuance until it felt as if it were instinctive, second nature, even supernature. But you did it, and when you were finished, you found you had crossed a line; you knew you could be that kind of obsessive, could be the kind of person who lost days and nights over the slightest change, infinite possibilities with never enough time to fulfil them.

The banner quote high on the entrance wall for the exhibition: 'I'm interested only in expressing basic human emotions…', said Rothko.[1] Contrast it with Giorgio Agamben (on Bonnard), 'I saw that colour—which is the form of ecstasy—is also intelligence and constructive reason'.[2] And Jean-Luc Nancy, writing about listening, says 'timbre opens, rather, immediately onto the metaphor of other perceptible registers: color (Klangfarbe, 'color of sound', the German name for timbre), touch, taste, even the evocations of smells"'.[3] But in the reverse, what is the sound of colour, the touch, taste, scent of what surrounds me? What is one is necessarily the other, because obsession demands saturation: the possibility of filling every sensory space with its presence which leaves us with nowhere to go but to it and ourselves in varied aural, oral, olfactory, gustatory, tactile dimensions. I wish I could tell you I

[1] From the Mark Rothko exhibition at Fondation Louis Vuitton, Paris, December 2023.

[2] Agamben, Giorgio. *What I saw, heard, learned . . .* trans. Alta L. Price (London, Calcutta, New York: Seagull Books, 2023), 34.

[3] Nancy, Jean-Luc. *Listening*, trans. Charlotte Mandell (New York: Fordham University Press, 2007), 42.

am a synaesthete but I am not; the entirety of this exhibition, and so too this essay, is haunted by Ormonde Jayne's Xi'an, its nutmeg and rhubarb, musk and sandalwood the equivalent of olfactory plumes of holy incense, nuance and shadow.

This is the point of it: obsession reduces the universe to these two things, which in contradictory turn reveal their vastness. Intrusion and reflection. Contraction and expansion. The former: Ian Penman says in *Fassbinder Thousands of Mirrors*, 'in many of Fassbinder's 1970s films we find the garish colour schemes of the new consumer society run riot. As if everyday life were itself drugged.[4] Rothko bleeds into *World on a Wire* (1973)—made for television—an unmistakable presence in the vivid orange, blue, and pink blocks and lines of the claustrophobic future's background. And the latter: taking in Rothko becomes the sensory and cerebral equivalent of free diving, an extreme meditation. The immersion into the obsessional colours of *No.16* (1951), with its blurred block of forest green set in green-shadowed gold, or the censorious grey-blue-black stripes of *No.5* (1949). In an essay by Eleanor Nairne, she quotes the artist:

> The whole problem in art is how to establish human values in this specific civilization.

And,

> My . . . pictures are involved with the scale of human feelings the human drama as much of it as I can express.[5]

The new worlds of Fassbinder and Rothko are ones of revelations and redactions; to emerge knowing we found something of ourselves within. But it is also the case that sometimes, we find that we were never there; that too, is revelatory.

On the train through France, Belgium, and the Netherlands, I have been reading the Penman book; between this and the exhibition, it solidifies the idea of intrusion and reflection as symbiotic, as if the secret of life lies in these poles of obsession. The obsession with someone else and their obsession. The obsession with wanting to be saturated by the things which possessed them; not exactly mimesis, but the colour chart keeps coming back to mind: where does one fit into someone else's colour scheme? What tone or nuance are we, and what do those particular shades represent? It is not as easy as thinking, *I am a chameleon, all that is required of me is to be in juxtaposition to them and their work*, our biological pigments arranging themselves accordingly so that we become the thing we are witnessing. According to a 2014 article:

> An excited chameleon might turn red by fully expanding all his erythrophores, blocking out the other colors beneath them. A calm chameleon, on the other hand, might turn green by contracting his erythrophores and allowing some of the blue-reflected light from his iridophores to mix with his layer of somewhat contracted yellow xanthophores.

If only we could move through life with such seamless emotional transition. Christopher Isherwood suddenly comes to mind: 'I am a camera with its shutter open, quite passive, recording, not thinking'.[6] No. This is the logic of the irritated fellow exhibition-goer, though in a way I understand and empathise with the sentiment. It is the safety of the distance of observation, the removal of the self in the presence of possibility that becomes desirable over the thing itself. But if we choose otherwise, we learn to expand and contract our senses and emotions in the face of fear and impossibility; a simultaneous capturing and adaptation which shows us that obsession lies somewhere between the chameleon and the camera. Regardless of our choice, Rothko's canvases become the tangible embodiment of Freud's psychic topography.

[4] Penman, Ian. *Fassbinder Thousands of Mirrors* (London: Fitzcarraldo, 2023), 56.

[5] Eleanor Nairne, "The Friction In Between," in *Mark Rothko 1968: Clearing Away* (London: Pace Gallery, 2021), 35.

[6] Isherwood, Christopher. *Goodbye to Berlin* (New York: New Directions, 2012), 3.

I spend more time sitting down in front of the sometimes wall-to-ceiling expanses of Rothko's canvases than I do standing. When I stand, I am more often than not leaning back, pressed against a corner so that I might take them in in multitudes, a deliberate oversaturation—overdose—of colour and emotion. Still, there is no escaping that to take them in means the horizons of his work are consistently broken by the insistent verticals of restless bodies passing to and from. The broken always emerge. I am trapped in *No. 5/No. 22* (1950) for some time, lost in the fine, almost out-of-character white lines which interrupt a wider stripe of red enclosed in an almost artificial orange and shades of mustard yellow. A chart, a measurement, a path . . . this is obsession. To follow a broken line, thinking it will nevertheless lead you to a place you want to—need to—go.

Take a picture and move on. I am a camera. This is the slightly mocking inner voice that interrupts my reveries, my hands gripping the bench or clenching in my coat pockets before I think again of colour charts and chameleons, of what René Girard refers to as 'mimetic desire: you desire some thing because someone else does. That person's desire, in turn, is reinforced by your desire'.[7] This circle of obsession is almost violent: in my head I am moving from colour fields obsessed by emotion to the numbered fragments of Penman's obsession of a man obsessed with cinema, to Girard's telling of the projection of Salomé's mother's obsessional desire for revenge onto her daughter. *Bring me heads and emotions, colours and images. Bring me possibilities*. My desire is both born from and borne on infinite desiring, and so the cycle continues.

Penman: 'it's not the idea of total surveillance that is so frightening as the sub rosa implication that we might all secretly desire such a thing'.[8] It is hard to ignore the obvious in an exhibition, but here in this one, more so, where the artwork is so abstracted, devoid of characters and narratives outside of the beholder's mind. I am watching people look at paintings while security is scattered through the rooms watching us. I am looking at the security people and wondering what goes through their heads, if anything, beyond their specific instructions. In quite a different way, we are all obsessed here: on watching and looking and the performance of them, if we are not actively and directly engaged in them. This is a fractured panopticon, but a panopticon nevertheless, and not an untrue measure of self-perception, of others, and of the aesthetic. What irony is there in knowing that what should be the openly sensory is also openly suspect in such a place? Surveillance lives and breathes on the oxygen of others; again, we are expanding and contracting in this space in multiple ways, multiple obsessions.

I was startled on seeing Rothko's quote on entering the building, having had used it in my own book on Michel Leiris and Édouard Manet's *Olympia* as a reference to the erotics of modernity and destruction. Somehow this reminder brought his reds into sharper focus in person, partly from knowing I had been bleeding again; with it, another possibility gone—not usefully over a canvas or a page it is true, but is there a difference between a red of value and a red without? Vast blocks and swathes of it represent destruction, rebirth, and desire all at once, whether passive or active: Petra's cluster of scarlet flowers on a wide black ribbon round her throat and her painted lips in *The Bitter Tears of Petra von Kant* (1972), the red pompom on Querelle's sailor cap in *Querelle* (1982). Fassbinder collides spectacularly with Olympia, and so with Leiris and myself, which leads us back again to Rothko, bound up as we are in his ultimate reds: here are our essences, our cycles and desires laid bare on these walls, to read and listen, project onto. Obsession is, put simply, the infinite taking of an emotional inventory.

[7] Girard, René. *All Desire is a Desire for Being* (UK: Penguin Classics, 2023), 121.

[8] Penman, Ian. *Fassbinder Thousands of Mirrors* (London: Fitzcarraldo, 2023), 66.

KIRSTEN MOSHER

SPLIT-SCREEN

I have got used to the pause between the end of this and its beginning. The indistinct pixels marking dusk. Looping. The clarity of dawn.

Do dishes while waiting for the coffee to brew. Rewrite the opening scene, no longer the start. Suds. Both hands in. Cobalt blue patterns float, the plates sink. My mother's Persian dish set, now mine, a maze of remembrances. The tips of my fingers rub sound out of the clean surface, good to go.

I had described it all, already (me at the museum, the video, my mother). My phone is propped on the window sill over the sink, speaker on. Again, I ask José. He thinks he remembers it, but my description of the video has become so detailed, he isn't sure if he saw it, or if he just imagined seeing it.

I can't get it out of my head.

I pored over museum listings. It was part of a big group exhibition. I knew that. What was the name of the artist? Maybe I'd never noticed. Nothing matched my memory of the split-screen video.

I can still see the video covering one wall. The hum of the projector mounted on the ceiling. Dust caught in the stream of light it cast across the dimly lit room. The room, not that big. I was glad to be the only one there. The floor, carpeted. I had to put the headphones on to listen. One pair hung on a discreet hook to the right of the entry. Like you are supposed to be alone in the gallery. The room, open on one side to the main gallery, but still private feeling. It was the only quiet spot on the whole floor.

A woman narrated the story in the video (maybe the artist), her voice like a friend talking on about something, like she expects you to listen and when she's done talking it will be your turn to talk and her turn to listen. It kept switching back and forth from single screen to split-screen while she walked you through her day. She, in her bedroom, in a hallway, going to work, at her cubicle, at her desk, in the aisle at the mini-mart. The costumes she wore to do average things like taking the trash out, and the way the costume was hidden under her work-clothes and how part of the costume was dangling out the back of her skirt and the way she tucked the orange and black spotted leopard tail into her underwear.

I try to recall specific works from the other art exhibits that day. I can't. Why can't I? I try jogging my memory. I circle back to being in the room with the video projection, back to the split-screen, how hot it had been, slipping my flip-flops off. The muted tones of the carpet, soft feel.

Standing in front of the video, I was on the phone with my mom. There were so many calls between us at that time, they all seem to blur into each other. But I remember this call. I was rambling on to her about the exhibit. I was describing the video from start to finish. Did I mention the artist's name? Would she remember it if I had mentioned the artist's name? Her memory is blurring, remembering her childhood like it happened yesterday, the time her sister caught a fly between two fingers and swallowed it without blinking, then not remembering the details of the last ten minutes, what I had said.

(If she could even remember the last ten minutes—she goes back and forth between years, writing lists. She reviews her address book for clues.)

Her address book. She's had it for so—It's old. There's the letter M. Who is listed under M.? Family members. Me. My old address. And underneath, my old-old address. She wants to cross them out and put in my new address. No. She doesn't want a lot of cross outs. Everyone has a cell phone but her. She has to write everything down. She writes on scraps of paper when she can't find the notebook. Her scraps of paper are piling up. She can't find her Today list. The Today list will say 2 pm. That's when her daughter (me) will call. She looks for a pen. She writes, *Don't complain about the blue sheets.* She doesn't like her blue sheets. Not everything needs to match. She doesn't want to seem ungrateful. She would have preferred white sheets. She only watches *Blue Planet*, skips over the screechy jungle stuff. She wonders what R is doing now. She'd rather listen to whales. Watch the whales bump up against the screen of the television. She can't reach the mute button. The phone is ringing. She drops the receiver then fishes it back off the floor with its curly cord.

(I remember calling her back, conversations blurred, bits splicing back and forth.)

Hi Mom! Yeah, I'm at the museum now. Yes, it's already two o'clock. I'm the only one in the gallery. I know! It sounds like we are in the same room.

I wish you could be here too. Yeah, like when we used to . . . I am going to describe the art now. Yes. Every detail. Remember our deal? My eyes/your eyes, until

The exhibit? It's all video. We're in the middle of the loop. Yeah, there is audio too. The galleries are all carpeted, to make it quiet. I wish I could take my flip-flops off. Don't worry Mom, I wouldn't do that.

I got half my earbud dangling, so I can talk to you on the phone, and I'm holding half the head-phone up to my left ear for listening to the video. There's nothing else in the room. Just the video. It's projected on one wall. Yeah, the video covers the whole wall. The wall is the screen. Right.

It shows a woman lying on a bed, but it's not nighttime. You can see the sun shining in, maybe she's just taking a break. Oh, she's starting to masturbate.

Sorry. What kind of sheets? They're white, like everything here.

No, she's funny, saying she just wants to get-off, to climax, that she needs to release a fuck-lot-of-tension. What?

Your sheets? I gave them to you.

Sea blue, they're going to match your walls. You said you wanted to paint your walls blue.

Well, the walls in the video are white, they blend in with the

I know. Mom, it sucks to be stuck at home. Did Ari come in to fix your lunch yet? Wait, now she is saying she would rub herself anywhere, like at work sneaking under her desk, so funny.

I know, I know, you are a cool mom, remember when we saw *Vagina Monologues*?

Ha, yeah, not shocking.

So, she's saying she masturbates in bathroom stalls or even just in public, like all she has to do is think about it. Now the video is cutting to some guy on top of her. The screen is split in half. One side shows her in her bed and the other

I don't know. Maybe she's in a hallway, her cheeks are pressed down on the wall. Sorry Mom, I can't today. How about take-out next time I come up to visit.

Shush, I can't hear

She's saying that he

No Mom, she's not naked. I mean, actually her skirt is pulled up. That's on the right side of the split-screen with the man, but she is wearing jeans on the left side of the screen where she's on the bed. Now she's turned over on the bed, copy-ing the position she's in on the right side of the screen, with the man, so she's doing the same thing on both sides, but on the left side, on the bed, the man's not there.

Mom, he's not on the bed with her. It's like the video edits are showing a memory. She says she needs to think about what happened to get to cli-max, like it's the only way she

Um, the Kandinsky show was last month? Right, the memory is like a formula. Now all she has to do, is the positions, remember how he forced her to

Do you have *Blue Planet* on? It sounds like you've got monkeys in there with you. Can you turn it down? The woman is just saying that she needs him. She needs the memory of him shoving her

So that's the stuff that's happening on the right side of the split-screen, to help her relieve the pressure that builds up in five-or ten-minute increments throughout the. No, he's not on the left side, he's not in her room.

No, nobody's in the gallery with me. I'm alone. Uh, right Mom, the right side of the split-screen

(And then I tried to tell my mom that the man was raping the woman. But she was talking while I was talking, turning the volume up on the TV instead of turning it down, saying that she thought the remote was broken.)

That moment in the gallery, during the silence between the end of the video and its restart, I felt elated. My spine straight, electric-charge. My ears ringing, room suddenly larger. The feeling stayed with me as I wound my way out of the maze of art objects and museum visitors.

I couldn't stop thinking about the video, the artist. She was funny and alienated and powerful. She consumed public spaces, wore costumes and shot the video making sure that the glare in her bedroom was just as bright as it was when she was out on the sunlit street catching the bus to work. She, Master of the Universe, masturbating in public spaces, re-mixing her most painful memories—then (as I imagine it) in the constant context of claiming her sexuality, editing her videos in a dimly lit room, splitting clips and jamming them back together.

Sometime after that visit to the exhibit I was pacing in front of a marble statue of a naked man daintily touching his chest in the Greek and Roman Hall at the Metropolitan Museum of Art in New York. I was on the phone to my mom, telling her about the exhibits, and trying to convince her not to have the house painters repaint her house for the third time in two months. They were taking advantage of her lapses. She hated the most recent color. She thought something else would be better.

By the time I arrived at Mom's house for my weekend visit, it had already been repainted. She was nervous about her choice. I said I loved it. She was so relieved. At that point, I would have said I loved any color she chose. But I really did like it. I asked her what the specific name of the color was, like what it said on the color chip. She didn't know. She asked me to walk around the house so I could admire it properly. I did. I kept my eyes fixed on the color. Not a trace of the previous coats of paint remained.

That evening I found myself rummaging around her basement looking for leftover cans amongst the brushes and drop cloths. But the names on the cans were smudged with paint, references gone. I stood there, thinking back to the brief silence between the end and the restart of the video, before climbing the basement staircase to rejoin Mom by the TV.

Thomas Walton

Unsavory Thoughts

Don't Tell Me Your Dreams

My friend knows everything about his dreams. That is, he knows what they mean. Every event that occurs, he finds a meaning for it, and he'll go on and on about what he dreamt about and what it means.

I don't mind having dreams, but I don't like talking about them. And I absolutely abhor anything resembling dream interpretation. I'm glad I didn't live in the mid 20th century. All that Freudian, Jungian pseudoscience . . . yuck, horrible. Even when my wife—whom I love—starts to tell me about her dreams, I immediately feel claustrophobic. It ruins the morning for me. I leave. I leave because if I don't leave, I get irritable. I know myself. I despise talking about dreams.

Sometimes she—my wife (who I love)—tells me about her dreams before I have a chance to get out of bed. First thing in the morning. I'm not even really awake yet. As consciousness dawns on me, I realize she's talking about her dreams. I'm trapped. By the time she's done describing them, I can't hide my distaste.

"What's wrong?"

"I've told you before," I say, apologetically, "I can't stand talking about dreams."

"Why not?"

"I don't know."

"Well what did you dream about last night?"

"Nothing."

I always say nothing, even if I've had the most wonderful dream. I don't want anyone to tell me what my wonderful dream *means*. I don't want anyone even knowing what I dream—even my wife (who I love). My dreams are my dreams. In a world where there's less and less privacy, dreams are about the only place where no one can see you. No phone is listening. No one's overhearing. No data's being gathered. And no one is commenting.

I like to think of dreams as if they are a snowfall when it's warm, when it's forty degrees: they just appear, flurry about, then melt away. That's a perfect dream interpretation, one that doesn't interpret at all. There's no need to ask, "what did it mean when the flakes blew this way, that, when they swirled up into the streetlight, or fell fast and heavy onto the drive?" Who cares? Were they beautiful? Yes. Terrible? Yes. Did you slip on the ice? Yes. That's it. Leave them alone.

To reveal your dreams on a regular basis (as my friend does) shows, I think, an incredible amount of narcissism. We live in an overly revealing society. Why does everyone think their experience is so interesting? The exhibitionism long ago reached embarrassing proportions. It's something like a nudist on the beach . . . it may feel good to you to be naked but that doesn't mean other people want to see it. Why do you need to reveal yourself to enjoy being alive? Show some discretion. Some taste. Grab a towel for gods sakes!

With respect, my dreams are my dreams, and yours are yours. I'd like to keep it that way if you don't mind.

Let Me Tell You a Dream

My grandparents owned a timeshare in Fort Meyer's Beach when we were kids. My brother and I played tennis there. They had a small condo in a huge building. They didn't have it very long, but I remember going there a few times. In spring, I guess. Or maybe summer. We drove down from Milwaukee in a brown station wagon. People didn't fly as much, then. If you had a station wagon, you took that.

I had nightmares when I was a kid. I still have nightmares. I never tried to figure out why. My mom says she has nightmares, too. I guess I got them from her, if you believe in that type of thing—the passing down of nightmares from one generation to the next. I suppose that "the passing down of nightmares from one generation to the next" is one way of looking at the history of humanity.

In one of the dreams recently, someone was tearing my dictionary apart. I couldn't tell if he was doing it intentionally. He was just letting it fall apart. And it did fall apart. It was falling apart. I watched, helpless. It doesn't sound like much, but I assure you it was terrifying.

My brother and I weren't very good at tennis, but we had energy. Endless energy. What we lacked in skill, we made up for in spite, in determination, and a competitive hatred only known to brothers. We may have been from a family whose grandparents owned a timeshare with tennis courts, but we were not from a family who took tennis lessons. We were self-taught. We willed the ball over the net. Often we just hit it as hard as we could, hoping it might hit our opponent in the face. We would take turns being John McEnroe and Bjorn Borg. My brother was blond and actually looked like Bjorn Borg. I had the mouth of McEnroe. The tennis matches usually ended in a fight.

At one point in the dream, a former neighbor of mine who'd been kicked out of his apartment tried to run me over with his motorcycle. He blamed me for kicking him out, which was somewhat fair since (1) I manage the building where he lived, and (2) I was the one who posted the eviction notice on his door. The dictionary was now in shreds. I was able to avoid my former neighbor for most of the night, but eventually he succeeded. Eventually he just ran right over me. Nothing ever hurts in my dreams. Things just happen.

My grandparents were of the country club age. Born in the twenties. They came of age during World War II. Perhaps the country club age was a coping mechanism for the horrors of the atomic age, the mass-killings of the war, and the tense, uncertain future of the Cold War on the horizon. The country club as antidote for existential crisis.

My grandparents golfed and bowled and played bridge and pinochle right through Vietnam. My father got married, had all four of his kids before the war in Vietnam was over. His draft dodger's capital was high. He was white, married, had four kids and a sports hernia. He wasn't drafted. I suppose he could've volunteered, but maybe the hernia would've kept him out?

The dream lasted all night. It's difficult to describe. Dreams are like action movies to me. They don't make any sense. They're just a series of fights, murders and screaming. And there's never enough sex.

It was 1980-something. The early 1980s. When we were in Florida playing tennis. I was ten or less. My brother was two years younger. My sisters were three and seven years older than me. They were never around. Sometimes I think about that. About how I never knew where my sisters were. At least until I went through puberty. Then I always knew. That is, if one of their friends was over, I always knew. Then I just hung around them, or tried to, with no idea what to do or say. I wasn't sure why I was even hanging around.

After he ran me over, he grabbed an iron poker. In my dream the iron poker was called an andiron. I remember that very clearly, the word andiron. Even though it wasn't an andiron, it was an iron poker. Anyway, the former neighbor of mine grabbed the iron poker and crushed my skull with it. He kept crushing and crushing my skull. I watched from a tree branch nearby. It went on long after I was dead. Most of the times when I get murdered in my dreams, the murder continues happening long after I'm dead.

They would take us to play miniature golf. For a long time I thought miniature golf only existed in Florida. We said "miniture" golf. Three syllables, not four. I liked miniture golf, but even as an adolescent I found some of the holes a bit overthought.

Overwritten. They were just trying too hard to be witty, those holes. It wasn't curiosity that killed the cat. An excess of design killed the cat.

When I came down from the tree (more like a rat than a bird or human), I walked past my former neighbor, who was still engaged in my destruction, still thrashing me with the poker. (The poker, I might note, was *not* red hot. It wasn't hot at all, though it was red from all the blood everywhere. I realized this in the dream—the fact that the red poker was not a red-hot poker—but only as a trivial piece of information, a sort of subtext.) I walked past him and down the stairs to the subway. In the subway there was a kid, something like my tennis-playing self, who began antagonizing me. I told him to leave me alone, but he wouldn't. He kept saying, "You want me to cut you? You want me to cut you, don't you?" "No," I said, and I called 9-1-1. The dispatch put me on hold. While I was on hold the kid reached around my back and cut me. He cut me badly. My skin and muscle splayed open easily, like a fish. In the dream I even smelled fish. My open body smelled like fish.

I tried to hold the kid off with my free hand while holding my phone with the other. He reached around again, and sliced me open again. Blood was spraying everywhere, and I was furious with 9-1-1. I decided to give up, I hung up. The phone wouldn't fit in my pocket, though, and while I was trying to shove it in, the kid sliced me open again.

I still liked playing minuture golf, even though the holes were overdesigned. My brother and I would hit the ball and see if we could "accidentally" get it to roll all the way out into the street. My grandfather found this unamusing. The last hole on the course, the one that steals your golf ball and somehow (pneumatically?) returns the ball to the office, always made me sad. Each time we played I would experience a tremendous sense of loss when we reached the last hole. Of grief, even. And also a vague sense of being duped. For this reason, I always feel tricked when someone close to me dies. When I think of divinity personified (which I don't, really, but when I do), I always think of a Jester.

A train came then. We were in the subway. It was an express. It didn't stop. Faces in the windows sped by me. I thought they would see me and try to call 9-1-1, but the faces just stared, bored, while the kid cut me again and again and I tried in vain to put the phone in my pocket. I had been dead for a long time, but the kid kept carving me. It was the second time I died that night.

Tennis was popular in the 80s, mostly because of Andre Agassi. He was young and cool and everyone loved his hair. His hair was the same as John Stamos' hair, but blond. My sisters had a huge crush on him. On both of them. I tried to grow my hair out but it didn't look very good.

Then I was suddenly *on* the train. The train was delayed and we were just sitting there. I could see me on the platform. I was already murdered but the kid kept cutting me. He had scissors now like those pizza scissors they give you at Neapolitan-style pizzerias. I looked out at me already murdered, a pool of wet meat on the platform floor, and the kid on his knees working at me. Cutting me into bits and then sewing parts of me to other parts. I don't know where he got the needle and thread.

I miss my grandparents. I loved the way they drank gin, and moved slowly across the room with martini glasses in their hands. They had a Cadillac with leather seats and sometimes I can smell it. And sometimes when I smell a tennis ball I think of them, too. And the minuture golf AstroTurf. When I see AstroTurf I think of them. And how hot it used to get on the tennis court in Florida.

When the train went into the tunnel, I suddenly saw my reflection. I don't know why but that was the most terrifying part of the dream, my reflection. I went from watching me being cut up and sewn back together, to seeing my face staring back at me. When I saw myself so close, I gasped and immediately woke up.

Henry Wessells

Moby-Dick and American Literature of the Fantastic

or, Bound for the South Seas

Prologue

This is a crackpot theory with a kernel of truth. It requires some minimal familiarity with the works of H. P. Lovecraft and Herman Melville. It took shape as I re-read *Moby-Dick* for the first time in decades in January 2016, and I first expounded it at the California Antiquarian Book Fair in February 2016, to my friend Bill Reese, a supreme Melville collector and the greatest Americana dealer of his generation. Great reader though Bill was, he had never read *any* H. P. Lovecraft and so he greeted my geste with the glazed look that means, as any performer will tell you, you have lost your audience. On another occasion, an eminent Melville scholar responded with a Jupiterian frostiness. So you have been warned. I performed early versions of it with impromptu embellishments a few times in the interim in bar-rooms and one evening on the patio at Readercon in Quincy, Mass., for Jim Morrow and a few others, in July 2017. This final text was read at Readercon in July 2023. As you will see later, it is necessary to give this chronology.

Ernest Hemingway was only half right: American literature springs from one book, but that book is *Moby-Dick* (1851).

I

Melville gives for the first time voices to the voiceless, to those who had heretofore been mere furniture of narrative. It is Tashtego, the "unmixed Indian from Gay Head, the most westerly promontory of Martha's Vineyard" (122)[1], who first names the object of the Pequod's quest:

"Captain Ahab," said Tashtego, "that white whale must be the same that some call Moby Dick." (166)

The cabin boy Pip dances at midnight in the forecastle until a squall arrives and the "jollies" are sent aloft to reef the topsails. "It's worse than being in the whirled woods, the last day of the year! Who'd go climbing after chestnuts now? But there they go, all cursing, and here I don't." (179)

Stubbs berates the elderly Fleece for overcooking his whale-steak and bids him preach to the sharks worrying the carcass alongside the ship. Fleece concludes with a mutter, "I'm bressed if he aint more shark than Massa Shark himself." (306)

II

Moby-Dick also marks the point where English poetry becomes American literature. To take three examples, here is Samuel Taylor Coleridge's "Rime of the Ancyent Marinere" transformed:

An intense copper calm, like a universal yellow lotus, was more and more unfolding its noiseless measureless leaves upon the sea. (320)

Melville had earlier named Coleridge and the albatross to assert Nature's precedence over the English poet. (191)

Chapter 93, the episode of Pip's loss overboard, takes its title from William Cowper's poem of madness, "The Cast-away", and its substance from these verses: "We perish'd, each alone: / But I beneath a rougher sea, / And whelm'd in deeper gulfs than he."

---

[1] All citations from *Moby-Dick* are to the University of California paperback with illustrations from the Barry Moser Arion Press edition.

By the merest chance the ship itself at last rescued him [. . .] Not drowned entirely, though. Rather carried down alive to wondrous depths, where strange shapes of the unwarped primal world glided to and fro before his passive eyes; and the miser-merman, Wisdom, revealed his hoarded heaps; and among the joyous, heartless, ever-juvenile eternities, Pip saw the multitudinous, God-omnipresent, coral insects, that out of the firmament of waters heaved the colossal orbs. (424)

And, of course, it is the "Sea-change / Into Something Rich and Strange" from Ariel's song in *The Tempest*, that echoes in Ahab's words:

This is a pine tree. My father, in old Tolland County, cut down a pine tree once, and found a silver ring in it [. . .] when they come to fish up this old mast, and find a doubloon lodged in it, with bedded oysters for the shaggy bark. Oh, the gold! (445)

So far so good, nothing extraordinary or particularly new about these citations. They are excellent passages. *Moby-Dick* is also a great and influential novel of cosmic horror.

III

To go ahead for a moment. The revival of interest in Melville during the 1920s is well documented, including a standard edition of his works, and the discovery of the manuscript of Billy Budd (first published in 1924). In France, Jean Giono read Melville and began a translation of *Moby-Dick* into French, eventually published in 1939. When the translation was to be republished by Gallimard in 1941, Giono declined to write a biography his publishers and instead produced a remarkable fantasia, *Pour saluer Melville*. It is a fictional interlude during Melville's visit to England in 1849 that bears directly upon the impulse leading Melville to write *Moby-Dick*.

Giono evokes a continual struggle within Melville:

Depuis quinze mois qu'il est dans le large des eaux, il se bat avec l'ange. Il est dans une grande nuit de Jacob et l'aube ne vient pas. Des ailes terriblement dures le frappent, le soulèvent au-dessus du monde, le précipitent, le resaisissent et l'étouffent. Il n'a pas cessé un seul instant d'être obligé à la bataille [. . .] s'il saute dans la balinière, s'il chevauche des orages de fer [. . .] il se bat avec l'ange. (38)[2]

Melville's unceasing fight with the angel, in the momentous night of Jacob where dawn does not come, is Ahab's struggle. Ahab can recall the domestic joys and tenderness of fatherhood, but once the *Pequod* sails he is intent and unwavering in his quest of the supramundane real, that which is beyond the barrier. He tells Starbuck:

All visible objects, man, are but as pasteboard masks. But in each event—in the living act, the undoubted deed—there, some unknown but still reasoning thing puts forth the mouldings of its features from behind the unreasoning mask. If man will strike, strike through the mask! How can the prisoner reach outside except by striking through the wall? To me, the white whale is that wall, shoved near to me. Sometimes I think there's naught beyond. But 'tis enough. (168).

And elsewhere:

"How dost thou know that some entire, living, thinking thing may not be invisibly and uninterpenetratingly standing precisely where thou now standest; and standing there in they spite?" (480–1).

IV

H. P. Lovecraft (1890–1937) was a native-born Rhode Islander, a cosmic materialist by philosophical inclination, and a writer of fan-

[2] Jean Giono, *Pour saluer Melville*. Paris: Gallimard, 1941. (See Author's Note below.)

tastic fiction. He lived for some years in exile in New York City. In August 1925, Lovecraft wrote down the plot outline for a story based on a dream from years before, and recasting an earlier tale.

In early 1925 Lovecraft dwelt in an apartment house in Brooklyn, and a neighbor was George W. Kirk, whom he had known since 1922. Kirk was a bookseller who later owned the Chelsea Book Shop on West 8th street in Manhattan. Sometime in the middle 1920s, Kirk gave a copy of *Moby-Dick* to Lovecraft, who recorded the gift on the book's fly leaf, and signed his name: H. P. Lovecraft, Esq., Providence, Rhode-Island.

I have examined that copy at the American Antiquarian Society. It has Lovecraft's fine fanlight window bookplate and bears a pencil accession note on the pastedown: Purchase S. Clyde King, Jr. Aug 8 '41. (King was a Providence bookseller). *Moby-Dick* was rediscovered in November 2017 (note that date) during a shelf read in the stacks. The book is otherwise unmarked. And yet, and yet.

"Let the owners stand on Nantucket beach and outyell the Typhoons." (483). In this passage from chapter 109 of *Moby-Dick*, I hear the origins of a phrase in a later story of Lovecraft's describing terrible events in rural Massachusetts, "The Dunwich Horror" (written 1928 and published 1929): *"some day yew folks'll hear a child o' Lavinny's a-calling its father's name on the top of Sentinel Hill"* (in *Tales*. New York: Library of America, 2005, page 375).

The horror in question is one of a pair of twins conceived by Lavinia Whateley in congress with Yog-Sothoth, an interdimensional being. Wilbur Whateley, uncouth and stinking, took after his human parent. The other twin did not.

After his return to Providence in April 1926, Lovecraft eventually completed the story he outlined a year earlier. "The Call of Cthulhu" was published in *Weird Tales* in early 1928. It is a globe-spanning tale of malign influences, primitive cults, and the resurgence of an ancient extraterrestrial being, Cthulhu (pronounced "khlul'-hloo"). In the subsequent decades, Cthulhu has stepped out of the pages of Lovecraft's story and, like Mary Shelley's monster, taken on a life of its own.

V

And so to the next step, the ambiguity of pronouns: "There she blows!" Invariably, throughout *Moby-Dick*. Elsewhere whales are "he," grammatically male by default, as buttressed by Melville's cetology and lore of the sperm whale fishery. And yet.

Moby-Dick is the intrusion of these terrible interdimensional forces into the ordinary. So ordinary cetology does not apply, and the white whale is a she-whale. In his last speech, Ahab proclaims, "Toward thee I roll [. . .] still chasing thee, though tied to thee, thou damned whale!" (574–5).

The fated rendez-vous is a hot date in the South Seas: Cthulhu is the spawn of Ahab and Moby Dick.

Q.E.D.

Author's Note

I had written an early version of this essay in the spring and summer of 2017; and then in December 2017, I learned that the American Antiquarian Society holds H. P. Lovecraft's copy of *Moby-Dick* (an edition published in Boston after Melville's death; the copyright notice is in his widow's name):

> Moby Dick or The White Whale / by Herman Melville author of "Typee," "Omoo," "White Jacket," etc.
>
> Boston : Dana Estes & Company publishers, [1892]. American Antiquarian Society copy has bookplate of H.P. Lovecraft. Inscribed: From George Willard Kirk, Esq. H.P. Lovecraft, Esq., Providence, Rhode-Island. Catalog Record #144128.

They wrote about the discovery:

14 November 2017

Fun fact: AAS has a copy of Moby Dick once owned by H. P. Lovecraft! A source of inspiration for him, perhaps?

https://twitter.com/AmAntiquarian/status/930549738360967168

It's a nice-looking copy too! [with illustrations]

https://twitter.com/AmAntiquarian/status/930550196295077893

Jean Giono, *Pour saluer Melville*. Paris: Gallimard, 1941.

> For the fifteen months since he has been at sea, he has been fighting with the angel. It is for him the momentous night of Jacob and the dawn does not come. Hard terrifying wings strike him, raise him above the world, tumble him, seize him again, and smother him. Not for a single instant has the struggle relinquished him. [. . .] when he jumps in the whale-boat, when he rides iron storms [. . .] he is fighting with the angel.

[This is my own translation; in the fall of 2017 (!) it was issued as a NYRB Classics paperback in an English translation by Paul Eprile.]

For George Kirk, see S. T. Joshi & D. E. Schultz, *An HP Lovecraft Encyclopedia* (Greenwood, 2001; Hippocampus Press, 2004), pp. 137-8.

Moby-Dick was not listed in the first two editions of S. T. Joshi, *Lovecraft's Library* (Necronomicon Press, 1980; Hippocampus, 2002), but is recorded as item 651 in the fourth edition (Hippocampus, 2017), "Gift of George Kirk," with citations to Lovecraft's letters and essays.

Marvin Cohen

The Historical Fox Hunt in Derbyshire

Words used to be appealing,
when my manuscripts mounted to the ceiling.
I used to be creatively fertile,
but now I'm only read by a turtle
that creeps between the different pages,
but barely gets anywhere in ages,
if he manages to get over the hurdle,
but he's slow at reading
despite my incessant pleading.
My writing is so ignored
that librarians assume I'm bored
and disgusted by elusive words
that assume only the toilet talent of turds.
I distinguish between verbs and nouns,
but they get entangled, like a fox pursued by
   hounds
that leap upon their prey,
but bark too much, so the fox won't stay.
All the hunters yell till they're hoarse
while riding upon their horse
to desperately stay the course.
All the hunters seem like perfectly English
   good guys.
Why all the pretense?
Due to the shy practice of self-defense.
Where did all those dogs go? Over the fence?
To recover them takes hordes of guineas and
   pence
and other fortunes equally immense.
To pursue the matter further is without
   sense,
so with all this I may now dispense,
but gather my words to condense,
which came from the netherland of whence.

Angela Townsend

Avoiding the Mayor

This is why I don't talk to you, Roy.

It's not that you asked for my hair the first time you met me. This is admittedly an unconventional way to welcome your new downstairs neighbor, but I have long been a harbor for the odd. You asked that, should I ever lop my locks, I entrust the leavings to you. In the variegated landscape of my life, this was not even a top-20 moment of farce.

It's not that you study the stickers on my Subaru. To festoon one's chariot with public declarations is to invite commentary, so you're only responding to my public service announcements. Yes, Vassar. Yes, really. Yes, "Love God and Love People." Yes, that is simple and difficult. Yes, WXPN is the finest radio station north of the Mason-Dixon line. Your blueberry-pie eyes glisten with spirits, with hints that we are kindred spirits.

It's not that you smoke ceaselessly from above, dropping fireballs that burn holes on my balcony. You have been here over forty years, and your habits are as old as your fixation on Florida. "Did you hear that someone got shot in Miami?" you yell down the stairs. "Did you hear about the bad apples on Daytona Beach? Do you like the Tampa Bay Rays? Do you have an Amazon Fire Stick?"

It's not that you clamor for my kindness, then cover it in Mod Podge and craft grotesque ornaments. "You got the diabetes, right? Does that mean you can't have much sex? That's what my gal told me. But I can't have sex because of my prostrate anyway."

It's not that you and your "prostrate" and the gallon jug of amber liquid that you tote back and forth across the parking lot are perpetually prostrate, brimming with tears that are not tears, craving in all directions.

It's not that the schizophrenic woman downstairs, the one who liked me, the one who was removed three months after I moved in, told me with clarion confidence that you were "a spy, like Nixon."

It's not that you fancy yourself the mayor of our languid condos, alert and akimbo on the third floor in your orange-striped shirts. When you are out of your cups, you miss nothing, which is a certain comfort. You invent atrocities — car theft at Building 2, unsavory characters gathering like a storm. But I have learned to separate the manticores from the manatees, the loneliness from the late-breaking news.

It's not that you feed the tame squirrels, dozens strong and daunted by neither human nor Honda nor hairy old mayor. I would never tell you this, but your squirrel care is my favorite thing about you. The execution is as odd as your limestoned face — one day a pyramid of vegan hot dogs, the next a bucket of pretzel nuggets — but your intention is admirable. Besides, I have long been a harbor for the odd.

But my waves churn when you come my way, Roy.

As a creature who fancies herself a collage of compassion and calico, I have guilt over this. Breakers and rollers of regret crash over me every time I scurry inside, pretending not to see you up there. You want to talk about Florida. You want to talk about Wheel of Fortune. You want to spin your wheels until you hear your baggy voice truly heard by other ears.

I want to be here for you.

But I live here, and you lean in, and I don't feel at home.

It's that you tell me tirelessly that we are doomed, a brittle John the Baptist who has long stopped looking for the One to come. Society is in free fall. There will be tornadoes tonight, and we will lose power for days. We are getting older, even me, and someday I will get sick, real sick, and at the end of each day we are all alone. Soon none of us will be able to afford spinach. Did I hear that Florida will probably snap off like a Slim Jim and sink into the sea?

I've spent a lifetime building my dinghy, Roy. I have heard the dark rumors, seen the sea maps that go black at the edge of the abyss. I have spent salty decades installing deck prisms, so even the deep downstairs has light. I have spied out hope's coves. The anchor holds. I cannot hold my peace when you throw fireballs at the sails.

I will throw you life preservers and rafts. I will gaze up at you with all the grace my eyes can muster. I will thank God for your secret heart and ask God to ease your roiling.

Maybe I am too self-protective. Maybe the day will come when I feel so much at home, not even a sodden eighty-year-old who wants my hair can stunt my selflessness. Maybe the squirrels will tell me gentle truths about you, and my harbor will open. But sometimes, Roy, I just can't talk to you.

Kurt Luchs

Lorca in the City That Never Sleeps

Federico Garcia Lorca's *Poet in New York* (*Poeta en Nueva York*) must surely be one of the most misunderstood and underappreciated books of all time. Written during his troubled sojourn in New York, Vermont, and Havana, Cuba, in 1929 and 1930, it was not published during his life (1898–1936) but only in 1940, four years after he was killed by Nationalist militia in Spain. Why did he not publish the book sooner?

Both the subject of these poems and their surrealistic style were foreign to him, that's true enough. However, it's a truth that doesn't really explain anything. Lorca had already made several sweeping changes in style and subject matter in his career, as any artist will do. These changes had led to his popular and critical success with the book *Gypsy Ballads* (*Romancero gitano*, 1928), a reimagining of the poetry and ballads of his native Andalusia. Yet he refused to be typecast in his poetry, his politics or his sexuality. He kept seeking new things to write about and new ways to write about them. Along with his ever evolving poetry, these creative impulses also found expression in his plays and drawings. These aspects of his artistry would not be fully embraced until after his death, something they have in common with *Poet in New York*.

Some of the poems that would make up the book were published in magazines first. To call the reception they received "mixed" would be putting it mildly. This no doubt contributed to the poet's apparent uncertainty and delay in issuing the book. When *Poet in New York* was finally published posthumously, the negative, dismissive critiques continued and reverberated for several decades.

I have my own theory about this. I think there are three elements at work here. First is the desire to put the artist in a little box called "rural poet of local color." This is the desire of the audience (and more shamefully, of critics) for the artist to keep painting the same picture, playing the same song, writing the same book. The second element of dismissal is more general, a rejection of surrealism overall as a legitimate technique. We are so over this rejection now that we have forgotten it ever occurred. But it did. Last but not least is that old favorite, the artist and his work being ahead of their time. Again, we tend to forget that this happens frequently.

As long as the horse of this ancient, unjust rejection is dead, why don't we go on beating it for a minute? Please bear with me as we dredge up some of these early, misbegotten critiques, most of which are hard to lay your hands on these days.

Poems of F. Garcia Lorca (Oxford University Press, 1939), translated by Stephen Spender and J. L. Gili, marked the first major appearance of Lorca's work in English. R. M. Nadal's introduction states about *Poet in New York*: "Although based on sincere feeling, the poem is loaded down with unsophisticated surrealistic extravagances, which, to my mind, spoil what might have been a great work."

The poet's own brother, Francisco Garcia Lorca, wrote in his preface to *Selected Poems of Federico Garcia Lorca* (New Directions, 1955): "If one thing distinguished *Poeta en Nueva York* from all his earlier books, it is the total absence of irony and humor . . ." Well, first of all, that's not even true. There is irony and humor there aplenty if you can accept it wrapped in surrealism, which, obviously, brother Francisco could not. Second, even if it were true, how would that invalidate a work whose primary emotions are shock and horror?

The South African poet and critic Roy Campbell was a complicated character for reasons we don't have time to go into here; still, T. S. Eliot and Dylan Thomas considered him among the best of his generation. His book *Lorca: An Appreciation of His Poetry* (Yale University Press, 1952) is worth tracking down, both for its critical insights and for a number of translations unavailable elsewhere. When it comes to assessing Lorca's New York poems, however, Campbell is just one more literary Helen Keller: "Lorca went and stayed in the U.S.A. for some time, but was unable to establish a real contact with the Americans or their way of life. The result on his poetry was entirely negative. He underwent while there the intellectual influence, if not domination, of Salvador Dali, his friend, who is also a great artist of international repute, but a far more complicated personality than Lorca, more resilient and aggressive, with a far wider range of sympathies and interests, and at home anywhere from the U.S.A. to Catalonia. Lorca attempted to follow the Catalonian into the complex world of surrealism, and lost his depth."

Ouch! It must be admitted that there is a valid point or two in this paragraph. Yet on the whole it underestimates and stereotypes Lorca, a complex person and artist in his own right with a wide range of sympathies and interests that don't always overlap with those of the more metropolitan Dali. So what?

Within a few short years the critical view of *Poet in New York* had shifted. Angel del Rio explains why in his introduction to *Poet in New York: A New Translation* by Ben Belitt (Grove Press, 1955): ". . . the situation had changed considerably: surrealism had been accepted as an expression of time's restlessness. Moreover, the tragic death of the poet, the defeat of the Spanish Republic and the shadow of war extending over the planet conditioned critic and reader alike to see in these turbulent pieces something more than a meaningless jabber." He then speaks of "the prophetic quality of the book.

Nearly two decades later Robert Bly expressed his unqualified praise for these poems in his commentary in *Selected Poems of Lorca and Jimenez* (Beacon Press, 1973): "The Spanish do not know what to make of *The Poet in New York*, and some critics consider it an aberration, or say flatly that it is exaggerated, or mad. Spain being still largely unindustrialized [note: recall that Bly wrote this half a century ago], they do not realize that it is an understatement. I think it is a marvelous understatement . . ." Bly also says, "His desire-energy becomes bottled up, grows desperate, and bursts out in wild images, poems of desperate power and compassion." He calls the result "still the greatest book ever written about New York." Need I add that I share this view completely?

The surest way to validate this opinion is to get to the poem we'll be looking at today, "Home From a Walk" (also sometimes translated as "Back From a Walk" and "A Walk Around"). My favorite translation of this poem is by Bly. Unfortunately, it does not seem to be readily available online. Several other translations and the Spanish original are available, so hopefully you can make do with them if you don't have Bly's volume of Lorca and Jimenez poems, which, frankly, you should.

The poem begins and ends with the same line, "Assassinated by the sky." There are only 12 lines, four in the first stanza and two in each of the other four stanzas. The poem is shorter than a sonnet, and, with its circular structure and each stanza ending with a long "o" sound in the original Spanish, it has its own kind of form. Of course, a long "o" sound does not constitute a strict rhyme scheme. Sometimes it's hard *not* to rhyme in Spanish. Additional form comes with the pairing of opposed images in stanzas two through four. Contrary to what the early critics thought, we'll see that the surrealism in these poems is quite apropos and sophisticated.

What a way to start a poem! "Assassinated by the sky." What does it mean? One of the most interesting things about this New York poem is that it doesn't mention a single objective, external, realistic feature of the city. And yet a very specific feeling about it is evoked—disturbing, nightmarish, hallucinatory. I take the opening and closing lines to be about the oppression a first-time visitor to the metropolis may feel with this endless procession of skyscrapers looming over him, blocking out much of the accustomed sky. Stanza one continues this oblique approach in its remaining lines:

between the forms that are moving toward the
    serpent,
and the forms that are moving toward the crystal,
I'll my hair fall down.

The references to the serpent and the crystal are enigmatic to say the least, strange if not quite surreal. But they are also very clear in a way. How so? Well, imagine you are riding a New York City bus. Would you rather it dropped you off at the serpent or at the crystal? That clarifies things a bit, yes? The last line of stanza one is perhaps Bly's most effective piece of translation here. Other translators have rendered the line as "I'll let my hair grow" or "I'll let my hair grow long" (the latter is how Ben Belitt does it). By putting it the way he does, Bly manages to bring out the tensions of opposites in the poem even more fully in English. Sure, you can let your hair down if it's grown long. The phrase also conveys, though, the idea of speaking freely and frankly, as well as the letting go of inhibitions. In effect, Lorca is giving his muse permission to run wild with surrealism for the next three stanzas.

Each stanza is a couplet beginning with the word "with" and introducing startling pairs of images. The first is "With the tree of amputated limbs that does not sing, / and the boy with the white face of an egg." The first image is of something natural and free, cut back to fit into an urban environment. Not to be too literal, but the lack of singing could be ascribed to fewer limbs and fewer leaves to make music of the breeze, as well as fewer birds to make their own music in the tree. This image of something natural cut back contrasts starkly with the image of the egg-faced boy. An egg is something that hasn't been

born yet, but here is this "boy" walking around as if he's an adult ready to face the city. He's not. And it may be that Lorca is partly referring to himself with this line.

The third stanza, with the second pair of contrasting surreal images, is: "With all the tiny animals who have broken heads, / and the ragged water that walks on its dry feet." The first image is terrible, despite being so generic. We have no idea what kinds of animals they are. It's enough to hear that all of their tiny heads are broken, presumably through some type of violence they met within the city. The opposite of these creatures with a central limb damaged beyond repair is something that shouldn't have any limbs at all, but does, the "ragged water that walks on its dry feet." This monstrous inversion of reality through surrealism turns benign, soothing water into a horror.

Stanza four completes the lineup of contrasting images and starts to move away from overt surrealism toward naturalism: "With all the things that have a deaf and dumb fatigue, / and the butterfly drowned in the inkpot." With the first image of the couplet, again, we have the very generic "things" suffering from an inarticulate fatigue. It seems these are not creatures but rather inanimate objects, which are not supposed to feel anything, let alone fatigue. The second image of the pair, the "butterfly drowned in the inkpot," seems fairly obvious. Who uses inkpots, after all? The butterfly would appear to be another stand-in for Lorca himself. He's projecting. The implication is that he should not be speechless, but he is, overwhelmed by what he experiences on a simple walk about town.

Stanza five, the final one, brings it all home. In the first line once more we have the image of something that should not be and yet is: "Stumbling over my own face that changes every day." How can he be walking on himself? I suppose he could be referring to his shadow. That would give the poem a Jungian tint, which, actually, I believe it does have. I also think he's saying that simply existing in New York is like trampling on your own humanity, your own face. No wonder it changes every day, and no wonder he ends with the same line that began the poem, topped off with an exclamation point for emphasis, "Assassinated by the sky!"

I realize this essay is already top-heavy with obscure quotes. Allow me the indulgence of one more from a favorite book, *Within the Context of No Context* by George W. S. Trow. He's responding to a *New York Times Book Review* interview with a woman novelist whose book imagines how the city could be improved. Trow says:

> Her idea was that New York should be *human*. Now, this is simply a mistake. New York is simply an inhuman machine put together to serve the most ambitious of a certain part of American secular society. It has human aspects, because human needs must be met before ambitions can proceed toward realization, but the fulfillment of those needs is an uninteresting precondition of the life of the ambitions. In human terms, there is no reason to live in New York . . .

That is the city Lorca wrote about so brilliantly, and that is why his New York poems were ahead of their time and probably always will be, like any genuine masterpiece.

KURT LUCHS

MIGRATION

The giant spiders are migrating again.
Their journey is long and perilous
because they can only travel in nightmares.
Last night as I dozed fitfully, two of them
came down the hill, and when they turned off Red Wing Avenue
I was able to blow out some of their dark, bulbous eyes
before the shotgun became black smoke rising from my hands
and a pterodactyl in a bus driver's cap
lifted me screaming into the sky.
Today, as I go about my business—
stamping ALREADY PAID on all of my overdue bills—
I can feel that it is they who sleep uneasily,
relishing yet also fearing our next encounter,
their jaws grinding, their unbearably hairy legs
twitching in anticipation.
This time there will be two shotguns
and a phosphorous grenade, and if all else fails,
a club wrapped in barbed wire at the big end.
Let your remaining eyes look upon that
and tremble, my dreamy darlings . . .

M.J. Nicholls

Very Progressive People

Every year, my husband and I attend the Hoxton Yachting Club's annual raffle and always leave empty-handed. In 2021, the top prize was a chrome-encrusted mizzenmast from Lester Yubb-Yubb, the world's premier aft enhancer, which went to the Forsythes who already own twenty-nine luxury sailboats and a million litres of the Adriatic. In 2022, the top prize was a ceramic reimagining of the Battle of Britain, recreated in painstaking detail by Vyvyan Whyte-Blyck and crisped in a special kiln at 556° F. These treasures—nor the consolation prizes of private boxes at Glyndebourne, invites to brunch at the Kremlin, or a quarter of a million pounds—ever seem to pass into our unworthy hands, no matter how many tickets we preorder months in advance.

This year, however, we were shocked and surprised to receive third prize, and extra shocked and extra-extra surprised when the prize offered to us was—brace yourselves for a surprise!—a negro servant. The crowd applauded somewhat half-heartedly when a strapping young black man, bald and muscular, the very spit of that chap from that Oscar-winning movie about moonlights or what have you, in a pair of chequered britches and tight beige shirt, came meekly toward us with a flat cap in his left hand, and stood by our side as the crowd swiftly turned away. At first I was mightily tickled and said "Very amusing!" to my husband Jeremy as the others awkwardly evaded our gaze and the raffle moved swiftly on. Our prize, whose name was Clarence, sat with us silently at the table for the rest of the evening and was not served any champagne.

Feeling rather awkward and unsure how to proceed, we cornered Dame Phyllis Norway, the organiser and deputy charwoman of the Royal Yachting Concern, who explained to us that Clarence was a real negro servant who had been kindly donated by an anonymous family in Hampshire, who no longer had need of any hired help, but would be paying his wages for however long we required his services. I readied myself to explain that Jeremy and I would feel rather ill-at-ease accepting such a prize in the current political climate, but I found myself reluctant to be a bother after such a pleasant evening, so we left the club with Clarence, who sat rather regally in the back of our BMW.

"Clarence, you understand we are very progressive people," I said to break the ice.

"Yes ma'am," he said.

"Oh, you needn't call me ma'am. Please call me Lorraine."

"Yessum."

"As I was saying, we are very progressive people, we think the Afro-British people contribute massively to our society, and some are in very prominent positions now, such as Trevor MacDonald or that portly chap in the Labour party."

"Yessum."

"I must say, what a fine American accent you have. Were you raised there?"

"No'm."

"Oh, I see."

The atmosphere remained a smidgen icky until we arrived at the house, where I showed Clarence to our daughter Pollyannabel's old (and very pink) room, apologising for not having prepared less feminine sheets, and provided him with a fresh towel and a pair of Jeremy's old pyjamas.

"Very grateful, ma'am. This'll do me fine."

"Good night, Clarence."

In bed that night, I had fevered conference with Jeremy.

"We can't possibly have a young negro servant following us around, think what this would do to our reputation for progressivism!" he said.

"We could actually use some help around the place, darling. Since Anneka left us we've struggled to find a regular cleaner, he might be a godsend, if he's willing to clean for us. Do you think he'd clean for us?"

"I'm not sure, do negro servants clean?"

"Don't call him a negro servant, Jeremy. It's black servant. And anyway, his ethnicity has nothing to do with it. Just call him a servant."

"Right, sorry."

"We'll check with him in the morning."

I slept poorly that evening, not because I was worried about having a strange black man in the house—his ethnicity was never an issue for me, you must appreciate our reputation in this regard—for example, Jeremy had recently raised the wages of two Asian chaps at his office, merely for doing their work ruddy well—but because I was concerned about the to-do that might result if he refused to do the cleaning. We invited Clarence to eat with us at the table that morning.

"I can take breakfast in my room, ma'am," he said.

"No no, we insist," I said.

He sat awkwardly at the table and accepted the omelette Jeremy had prepared.

"Listen, Clarence," I said, putting on the old Denby-Calton charm, "you should know we have nothing but respect for your people. What Martin Luther said about having a dream, where one day men would be hired based not on the colour of the skin but the content of their character, was one of the most powerful pieces of oratory of the 1970s. We don't want to do anything to make you feel uncomfortable, so we ask you, would you be willing to do the cleaning?"

"Yes ma'am."

"You wouldn't have a problem?"

"No, ma'am."

"And we might need you to pick up the shopping for us, and drive us around sometimes, can you drive, Clarence?" Jeremy asked.

"Yessuh."

"Please, no need to call me *sir*, Clarence!"

"Not yet," I said, with a wink.

"*Vivere in spe*, honey."

So, most unexpectedly, we found ourselves the owners, or should I say, the employers (although we weren't paying him—the keepers?) of a very retro servant indeed! We found Clarence a diligent and thorough operator, uncomplaining and obliging to a fault, and slowly our embarrassment at having a young black man speaking American street dialect in the house was nonexistent. When we were next at the Yacht Club, we recommended him to our friends.

"Once you overcome the initial squeamishness, the social taboo, they're actually very effective workers. You can see why those Southern families in America were reluctant to part with them before the whole civil rights thingy," I said to spinster Barbara Woolworth.

"But do you not feel awkward having him around all the time?" Marge Doughty asked me.

"Not at all. On his first day, we sat him down and explained that we understood the struggle of his people, Rodney Luther King and all that, so he didn't view us as modern-day plantation owners, whipping him into shape, how awful! Yesterday he broke a plate, and we didn't even dock the expense from his wages, although we don't control his wages. I wonder how much he makes, Jeremy?"

"Worth checking," he said.

Our recommendation slowly led to an upsurge in well-to-do families looking for black servants. Many recent asylum seekers from African countries were found, and swiftly recruited as live-in helpers.

"And if I may say so, they make for fine eye candy too!" I said.

"Oh, Lorraine, you vixen!"

Our story continues, and brace yourself for weirdness! As Clarence was cleaning around us we noticed his skin becoming increasingly black—not in terms of pigmentation—remember, we had learned as very progressive people to be colour blind—but in terms of the actual Pantone colour chart. Let me explain.

A week into his time with us, his skin had turned carbon-black, black in the sense the scientists understand blackness—the complete absorption of all visible light. Even when Clarence was stood in a shaft of sunlight, his skin was as black as the darkest cosmos.

A day later, we noticed his eyeballs, previously wide and bulging, and his thick protruding lips, had begun to dim.

The next day, they were scarcely visible, his sounds barely audible.

Later, we were unable to hear him at all.

Then his clothes began to absorb the blackness of his body.

Clarence, in the space of fourteen days with us, became an eerie void in the shape of a human being. His entire frame from top to bottom was black as black was black—*vantablack*, Jeremy learned was the blackest black known to man—as he hoovered the front room, polished the brass fittings, and featherdusted the bookshelves.

"What are we to do about him?" I asked Jeremy worriedly in bed.

"I don't know. We can't possibly dismiss him, we'd be accused of discrimination . . . you know, firing him for being *too* black."

"But he is too black. He's starting to absorb some of the furniture, have you noticed? When he was hoovering under the chesterfield, the backrest started fading to black in real time."

"Oh my, really?"

"Yes, and the hoover nozzle itself is completely black, as is the feather duster."

"I hadn't noticed."

"Honey, I had a terrible thought."

"What?"

"If we stand too close to him, could *we too* turn black?"

"Heaven forfend."

"Honey!"

"What? Oh, I didn't mean it like that, you know my progressivism on the race question. I meant that we don't want to ourselves turning into odd, human-shaped blackholes like this poor chap."

"I have a sneaking suspicion, you know, that this so-called anonymous family in Hampshire who donated Clarence to the raffle might be the Mercurats. You know, that mad scientist lot who were sued for conducting experiments on people?"

"Oh my, yes, that would make sense. I mean, there's no current scientific reason why a chap would turn completely black and slowly absorb everything around him, is there?"

"Not to my knowledge."

"I'll make some enquiries tomorrow."

The curious kerfuffle escalated before we could really knock our heads together. When I peeked into Clarence's room that morning, I found his bed had become a bed-shaped blackhole and the surrounding curtains and bedside tables were dimming too. Our tabby cat Eleutheria had been sleeping on his bed and had lost her charming stripy coat to become a black cat, or rather a blackhole of a cat.

"Good heavens, he's going to absorb the whole house!" I muttered to myself.

We had no choice. We had to have words with poor old Clarence that morning.

"Clarence, you know we value your work," I said, staring into the void that was once the handsome young black—lighter black—man, "but this metamorphosing into a blackhole business is really concerning us. I know you can no longer speak, but I hope you can understand me. I'm afraid we will have to let you go for the moment until we can get to the bottom of this. Do you have somewhere you can stay?"

He seemed to nod his head, if you could call it a head, or indeed if you could call him a him.

"I am pleased. Don't take this as a comment on the quality of your work, which has been exemplary, and I believe your previous owners—I mean employers—are still paying your wages, so you will not be out of pocket."

"We wish you all the best, Clarence," Jeremy said, showing him to the door.

As he vanished across the fields, a science-fiction blur vanishing up the narrow farm road to heaven knows where (we couldn't bring ourselves to drop him at the train station in case he absorbed our car), we returned to the kitchen for a stiff shot of whisky.

"I think that was the right decision, darling," Jeremy said, pouring me another.

"Those bloody Mercurats!" I fumed. "Taking a perfectly nice young boy and experimenting on him like that. I'll be having words with them, if we can ever track them down. Now everyone will think we fired him. Do you think we will lose our reputation for progressivism?"

"No, and anyway the poor chap can't speak, and no one knows he's turned into a blackhole. I think we should keep mum for the time being."

"Yes, probably for the best. Now, should we search for someone else, perhaps a nice Ukrainian lady fleeing that awful war?"

"I'll have a look tomorrow."

We never saw our prize, or what had become of him, again. A fortnight later, we read a strange story in the local paper that part of the River Osh near our house had turned inexplicably dark—all the waves absorbed into a Clarence-like void. I shuddered when I read it, I must say, but I suppose on balance, it's for the best, as long as the rest of that beautiful river is not completely depleted of all observable light. I also read later—connected, I am certain—that the Mercurats made a splash with their first so-called Humanish Helper, a person-shaped outline you could decorate with the colour of your choice, controlled by your laptop thingy, a silent servant that was set to revolutionise the world of domestic drudgery. It has to be said, I found the whole thing incredibly sinister. Those bloody Mercurats!

Aug Stone

Starting Out

"So," I declared. "I'm off to make my way in the world."

"Watch out for the big bat," he replied.

"The big bat?" I queried.

"The one that will knock you back down every time you try. Cracking your ribs while tickling its own. Not to mention the blows to your kneecaps, jugular, and the rearranging of your imagined good looks . . ."

"Oh," I scratched my right temple, ". . . I thought you meant the flying mammal."

"Well, there's that too."

Diego Lama

The Breakup

Translated by Rose Facchini

The mother had wanted two children, but years of desperate attempts produced only Pierpaolo. Perhaps because he was so coveted, Pierpaolo soon became a strange, spoiled, difficult, indecisive, doubtful, hesitant child: he didn't know how to make any kind of decision, as if two distinct and ungovernable entities co-existed within him.

He spent his life on the fence of absolute uncertainty until he turned twenty-two.

At the age of twenty-two, Pierpaolo was driving his new Mercedes at breakneck speed along a country road when all of a sudden, he found himself at a crossroads: I'll go right, he thought, no left, no right, left, right, left, right.

Although it wasn't a major accident, the crash was enough to snap Pierpaolo's neck, and he died instantly—no, on the contrary, he didn't die. His uncertainty plunged him into an everlasting and hopeless coma.

The emergency responders found his organ donor card in  his jacket pocket. In the operating room, they removed all his viable organs: kidneys, heart, liver, lungs, pancreas, intestines, bone marrow, corneas, brain, genital glands, arteries, veins, muscles, bones, and more.

The organs were transported by plane in two different containers to two different hospitals, one in Naples and the other in Turin. In Naples, they were transplanted into the body of twenty-four-year-old Piero (moped accident, no helmet), and in Turin into the body of twenty-year-old Paola (head-on collision between two cars).

Some years later, Piero and Paola met in Rimini.

On the beach, after they made love for the first time, they felt a strange attraction between the flesh of their bodies; as if fused together with sweat, they struggled to separate.

"I feel complete with you," Paola said to Piero.

"And I with you," Piero responded to Paola.

After three years, they broke up.

Their separation, which doctors studied with great interest, was dismissed as a normal case of chronic rejection by the immune system.

Don Zancanella

Ask Not What Your Country

1963: Julie 14, April 9, Ernie 5

Dad says, "We need to leave in ten minutes."

Julie is wearing her pink A-line shift and white shoes, as if she's going to church. April is on the couch reading, waiting for Mom to do her hair. Little Ernie doesn't understand where they're going or why.

"What do you think he'll say?" Julie asks.

"He's going to talk about conservation," Dad explains. "According to the newspaper anyway."

As Mom pulls April's hair into a ponytail, April says, "Ouch, not so tight," and then, "I hope it doesn't last too long."

Dad is pleased that this is an afternoon event. He delivers milk for a living and has to get up at dawn. If something's being held in the evening, he seldom chooses to attend. Ernie can't stop fiddling with his tie. He tosses it over his shoulder, then pulls it down again.

"We need to hurry," Dad says. "I'd like us to get decent seats. It's going to be a full house, what with school dismissed."

Mom herds the kids outside and Dad shuts the door. They've decided to walk because the auditorium isn't far and it's a glorious September day.

Soon other families join them, the Parkers and Tunbergs and Goffs. Julie hopes she'll run into some of her classmates. She knows this event is important because her parents and teachers say it is. Even though the president is Catholic, her mom voted for him; her dad didn't but her mom says, in a teasing way, "Your father is coming around." When Julie spies the Michaelsons, she says, "Can I walk with Patty?" Mom nods and says, "Of course."

Mom thinks this small town on the high plains is an excellent place to raise kids. It's safe and friendly and has a branch of the state university, which makes it seem special. If only the winters weren't so cold. Dad comes from an even smaller town. He served in the army and then came here to get an education, paid for by the GI Bill. But before he could finish his degree, the dairy offered him a full-time job and he decided school could wait.

Mom is holding Ernie's hand. "We're going to see the president," she says. Ernie's not the kind of child who's full of questions. Instead, he looks around solemnly, seeming to gather the world in.

Dad doesn't care much about what the president will say. He's more interested in the mechanics of the event. One of his customers said the secret service arrived yesterday to get everything ready. Dad wonders what "getting ready" consists of. How many people are involved? It seems like a waste of money, but it's hard to say since he doesn't know what they do.

April expects this to be boring and crowded. Crowds make her uneasy. She takes Mom's hand, the one not being used to hold onto Ernie, and watches Julie and Patty up ahead. The last time the schools closed for something other than a scheduled vacation was when they practiced what to do in the event of a nuclear war. "You have thirty minutes to get home," her teacher said. "However, you are not to run."

Dad's main complaint about Kennedy is that he's too good-looking. From his time in the army he knows that good-looking guys get away with things. But that's not the president's fault. It's simply how the world works.

"It's a lovely day, isn't it," Mom says. "Lovely," Ernie says, then repeats the word, "lovely, lovely, lovely," several more times as they walk.

Julie is envious of Patty. Patty's parents seem more interesting than her own. Her father teaches at the college, which she finds impressive, better than delivering milk. Patty says,

"There's Andrew." He's a boy she likes. Julie's not as boy crazy as Patty, so to remind her of this fact, she shrugs. Another thing Julie envies about Patty is her ability to do well in school. Julie's not a very good student. She finds most of her classes difficult and knows some teachers consider her slow.

They're almost there now. The atmosphere is festive. The high school band is playing on the lawn as they approach. Dad says, "Is Julie planning to sit with Patty? I think she should sit with us." Mom calls out to her. "Julie, come back here. You can see Patty again on the way home."

The more crowded it gets, the more uneasy April feels. She squeezes her mother's hand and sweeps the crowd with her large brown eyes. She'd have been willing to stay home with a babysitter but she wasn't given the option. With a babysitter and her cat. Mom often says, "You like animals better than people, don't you?" To which she replies, "What so weird about that?" There are lots of policemen, including one on horseback. That's something they've never seen before. Mom drops April's hand so she can pick up Ernie. These days he's almost too big to carry. As they approach the doors April reminds herself that somewhere inside the arena the actual president is preparing to speak.

1966: Julie 18, April 13, Ernie 9

People stopped having milk delivered so the dairy let Dad go. Now he works as a groundskeeper at the college, tending flower beds, mowing lawns, and in the winter shoveling snow. Mom has started working as a receptionist in a dentist's office. With both their parents out of the house, April watches Ernie. Sometimes they fight, but usually they get along.

Today they are at the lake, having a final swim before school begins. Julie is at a party on the opposite side. She was supposed to graduate last May but she missed too many classes, too many days, too many assignments and tests. Mom raged at her, Dad said, "Do as you please but

you'll live with the consequences." Julie said, in a voice too quiet for Dad to hear, "I hate you more than you know."

This might be Julie's last time with all her friends. Most of them have known each other since the first grade. Now some are going off to college and others already have jobs. Several of the boys have been drafted and will soon leave for basic training. Julie has started working as a waitress. The other women who work at the cafe are at least five years older than her. Simply by listening she's getting quite an education about work and motherhood and men.

When April takes Ernie to the lake, he likes to swim out to the floating pier and can spend an entire afternoon diving. At the beginning of the summer his best friend cut his foot on a jagged piece of metal. The cut got infected and incredibly, his friend died. Since then, Ernie has become even quieter than usual and prefers to be alone. Diving, shooting free throws on the driveway, and repeatedly reading the same two books. One is about a boy who moves to a new town and gets teased until he proves himself on the baseball team. The other is about building a settlement on the moon. As soon as he finishes the one about baseball, he starts the one about the moon again.

April worries about Ernie. Such a terrible thing to have your best friend die. She also worries about her older sister—Julie should have tried harder to graduate—and about her parents. Since her father had to change jobs and her mother started working, they argue all the time. April would like to stop worrying about her family but it's part of who she is.

Dad dislikes his new job. He hates his boss, and the work is hard for someone his age, getting harder every year. When he delivered milk he always felt as if he was his own boss, even though that wasn't true. Some days now he wakes up and thinks, "Is this all my life is going to be?" In the evening the television is always on, and he remembers when there was no television. Weren't things more peaceful then? One part of his job he does like is fixing the lawnmowers when they break. He wishes he'd become a mechanic twenty years ago, when he was young.

At the party, Julie gets wasted and throws up in the weeds. She's supposed to work tonight. She stumbles to the water's edge and walks out into the lake until she's in up to her chin. Then she drops to her knees. When she swims she usually shuts her eyes; now she forces herself to open them. The sun is a quivering presence, piercing the aquamarine. When she comes up she feels a little better. By the time she gets to the restaurant, she'll be okay.

Two nights later Patty comes in during her shift. Julie is embarrassed. Ten days from now she'll still be waiting tables and Patty will be living in a dorm at an out-of-state school.

"Oh hi," Julie says, puzzled to see Patty alone. "Is it just you?"

"No, I'm meeting Amy and Ben."

Julie blushes. "Oh. Well. You can sit anywhere. When do you leave for California?"

"Next Thursday. I'm so busy, I'm running in circles. You have no idea. How about that booth over there?"

When Amy and Ben arrive and join Patty, Julie asks one of the other waitresses to take their table. Then she hides in the kitchen until they leave.

Julie has only had this job for a few months but already she's tired of being a waitress. The boys her age, especially the ones who didn't do well in school, are getting sent to Vietnam. At least she won't have to do that.

1971: Julie 23, April 18, Ernie 14

Their parents don't stay together. It was obvious they were going to split up for at least a year before it happened. Both of them claim to have been the first to want a change.

Julie now lives in California. After Patty went there to school and came back talking about how

fabulous it was, Julie thought, fuck it, I'll go to California too. She hitchhiked west with a boy named Mark and now she's waiting tables in Fresno. Mark said he would pay the rent from the money he was making unloading trucks. Then one morning she woke up and he was gone. A few days later the police came to the door and asked her where he went.

"I have no idea. I didn't know him very well. He just disappeared."

"Didn't know him very well? What a load of b.s. He was living with you, wasn't he?"

"Is he in trouble?"

"Yeah, he's in trouble. Consider yourself lucky he's gone. You're a good-looking chick. I might give you a call."

California isn't as fabulous as Patty said it would be. Fresno is hot and dirty but Julie is too timid to try somewhere else. She'd go back home but life there would be no better. Actually, she doesn't know that. She'd like it if someone told her what to do.

April and Ernie now live with Dad. Their mother says she's not interested in raising teenagers. This makes April feel bad, especially for her brother. "Mom's just upset," she tells him. "I predict she'll change her mind."

Ernie looks up from the book he's reading and says, "I don't care."

April would like to go to college somewhere far away, but she worries about leaving Ernie behind. Dad doesn't mistreat them but he doesn't have much interest in them either. He gets home from work, eats by himself, and then watches TV in his room.

"What do you think, kiddo?" April says to Ernie. "Would you be okay here on your own?"

"I want to see the new Disneyland," he replies. He read about it in a magazine and now can't stop bringing it up.

"You mean Disney *World*."

"Yes. I keep forgetting what it's called."

"I don't know where we'd get the money. It would be an expensive trip."

Ernie changes the subject: "We should get a dog." He does this to annoy April, so she'll have to turn him down again. As if to put her in the position of being the mom.

"That's a terrible idea. We're bad enough at taking care of ourselves. Besides, if we get a pet, I'd want it to be a cat. I still miss Ruby. But answer my question. Would you be okay on your own?"

"Dad's here."

"Yes but . . . you know what I mean."

In the end April decides to stay in town for college and live at home. More and more, Ernie fills his time by reading. He doesn't really have any friends. At the school he goes to, everything social revolves around drugs. A guy he knows, Chris, is always saying, "Ernie, you want to get high?"

He shakes his head. "That's okay. I have to go home." The idea of taking drugs frightens him and he'd prefer to read.

One day he says to his father, "I remember when you delivered milk."

"Yeah, that was a good job."

"Did we get free milk back then?"

"No. We got a discount. Nothing's ever free."

This statement will stay with Ernie for many years to come. On the one hand it's a cliché. On the other hand it's an idea that can be tested again and again throughout one's life. This thing, this gift, this windfall, this moment of joy, this friendship, this love: How much did it cost?

April often tells him about her schoolwork. He senses she's doing it not only to be companionable but to convince him college is interesting. She says, "I'm writing a paper about JFK. Remember when we heard him speak?"

"Who?"

"President Kennedy."

He shakes his head. "No."

"I guess you wouldn't. You were only a little kid. His speech was about conservation, but the part I liked best had to do with how life is happier if you have a chance to use your skills to the utmost. He said that young people of the next generation would have a unique opportunity to improve the world."

"What do you mean conservation?"

"You know, taking care of the earth."

1980: Julie 32, April 27, Ernie 23

April and Ernie haven't heard from their older sister since Dad died. She didn't even bother to come to the funeral. He had a heart attack, an unexpected one. Now it's just the two of them living in the house they grew up in.

April finished her degree in accounting and works for a local firm. Ernie started college, stopped, started again, spent too much time drinking and taking drugs, and now seems to be doing better. A friend of Dad's hired him to work on campus, doing general maintenance—fixing broken windows, changing light bulbs, building shelves in professors' offices, that sort of thing. He still likes to read. He's very big on James Michener. The longer the book the better, as far as he's concerned.

In Fresno Julie is living with a guy. His name is Eli and he gets disability payments from the VA. She felt bad about not going to Dad's funeral but not bad enough to get time off work and spend the money to make the trip. She's jealous of April and Ernie for the extra years they had with him. She knows that's stupid—no one forced her to leave. Some people seem really family-oriented but not her. One thing she's done right is to avoid getting pregnant. Eli would suck as a father and she'd probably suck as a mom. Her own mother sends her a birthday card every year with ten dollars in it. A big spender, that's Mom.

One day, for no particular reason, Ernie decides to get in touch with Mom. She's now remarried and living in Florida. He locates her phone number and calls. Amazingly, she tells him he now has two half-brothers, six and eight years old.

She lives only a few miles from Disney World. That would have been more exciting news ten years ago. Now he doesn't care. Although if someone offered to pay his way, he wouldn't turn them down. He's read that there are adults who are obsessed with Disney World, who know everything about every ride and go there every year. To him that sounds strange.

When he tells April about his phone call with Mom, she starts to cry. "I remember," she says, "how she used to fix my hair."

Around that time, April starts dating a guy at the firm. She's only had a couple of boyfriends and thinks maybe it's time to get serious about someone, to get married and have kids. That's certainly what many of her friends have done. Occasionally, she reads an article about a new generation of women who value career over family, but she's seen little evidence of that. Maybe in big cities, among members of a certain class. Then she discovers the guy she's been seeing is seeing someone else.

After that she develops a case of eczema. It's not severe but it disturbs her to think it happened as a response to a guy who cheated on her. He's the one who should have gotten a rash.

1993: April 40, Ernie 36

April is going to Europe. She never thought she'd get the chance. A client of hers who manufactures a special kind of water pump is opening an office in Lyon. He wants her to set up his accounting system because he doesn't trust the French. She tells Ernie about it: "I'll be gone for two months but I guess you'll be okay here alone." "I'm a grown man," he says.

Julie died four years ago. They're not sure how. First they were told it was hepatitis and then some sort of stroke. All the information came from Julie's boyfriend Eli who seemed a little off. April said, "It's only us now, kiddo."

"Us and Mom and our two half-brothers," Ernie replied.

"True. But it's a little hard to think of people as being part of your family when you've never met."

"Do you ever wish you could pay them a visit?"

"I'm not going to make a special trip. If I had some other reason to go to Florida, I would."

"My theory is Julie died of an overdose," Ernie said. "I always thought we'd see her again."

April enjoys France. A river runs through Lyon and she likes walking along it, looking at the buildings on the opposite side. The food is as miraculous as everyone told her it would be, even in the most ordinary cafes. She doesn't have to speak French to do her job, but she forces herself to use the language whenever she can. By the time a month has passed she can converse a bit with strangers, an experience that leaves her feeling exhilarated. At night she lies in bed and replays each exchange.

Back home, Ernie is dating a girl named Carla. *"Woman,"* Carla corrects him, "You could call me a girl if I was sixteen." She too works on campus, in her case in the registrar's office, entering data into a computer.

"How'd you learn to do that?" he asks.

"It's just typing. There wasn't much to learn."

Like Ernie, she started college years ago but never finished. "This whole institution is staffed by people like us," he says. "Plenty of credit hours but no degree."

The first time he takes her home, he says, "I don't own this place. Well, actually I do, with my sister. But she's in France."

Carla looks around. "You have a lot of books," she says.

Before long she's staying with him every night. He's had girlfriends before but nothing like this.

He writes to April about her but doesn't reveal that Carla has moved in.

One day a man April works with says, "Do you know about the traboules?" Despite her improving ability to speak French, she thinks he said *troubles*.

"Do you mean in Ireland?"

He laughs and explains that the traboules are enclosed passageways in various parts of Lyon. In ancient times, their purpose was to allow the silk workers to carry their wares from place to place without getting rained on. Then, during the war, the passages allowed the residents of the city to evade the Nazis. He says, "Even today, one can use them to travel through the city without the risk of being seen."

April goes looking for the traboules and discovers it is as if a hidden Lyon exists beneath and behind the Lyon she knows. Winding corridors and concealed courtyards and a strange, covered staircase that goes up and up and up before connecting to a building that's invisible from the street. It's all quite intriguing and dreamlike. She returns again and again, finding new passageways and always stopping to gaze in wonder at the staircase. When April visits new places, she likes to imagine what it must be like to live there. To get up in the morning and ascend the mysterious stairs.

When her contract ends and it's time to return to the U.S., she tries to figure out a way to stay in France. Her only family is Ernie and she could fly home to see him every year or two—or, better yet, he could visit here. But she is unable to find a permanent position and not brave enough to simply live on her savings and trust that things will work out. How do people do it, she wonders, those who plunge forward without regard to the risks? Then again, that's what Julie did and look how she ended up.

Back at home she finds that Ernie's girlfriend is pregnant and they're planning to get married. "Oh, I'm so happy for you," she says and truly she is. She'd stopped imagining that either of them would get married and have children. Now people can stop talking about her and Ernie, that spinster and her bachelor brother who never left home. Ernie's girlfriend Carla deserves to be thanked for saving them, for preventing the two of them from succumbing to the inertia of a listless old age.

Ernie doesn't know what to say to April about the house. It was large enough for all five of them growing up but it won't be fair to Carla if his sister stays. Before he can figure out how to approach the matter, April says, "Just so you know, I'm looking for an apartment. I can't wait to have a place of my own."

When she's packing to move, Ernie comes into her room and they fall to reminiscing. April says, "Do you remember when we went to see Kennedy?"

"You always ask me that. I'm not sure. At this point I feel like I've heard you tell about it so many times that *your* memory has been inserted into *my* brain."

"We saw him in September of '63. He was standing up there talking and didn't know he had only two months to live."

"His speech was about conservation."

"See, you do remember." She tosses a pair of shoes in a box and says, "I'm forty-one and this is the only bedroom I've ever had—except in France of course."

"I feel guilty about making you move out."

"I'm fine. No one is making me do anything. I can't wait to be an aunt."

"Too bad when Kennedy talked about conservation nobody listened."

"What do you mean?"

"The polar ice caps are starting to melt. It has something to do with pollution and ozone. The earth is being cooked."

"Where'd you hear that?"

"I read an article."

"When you have a kid you won't have time to read so much."

"Don't you ever think about the future?" Ernie says.

"It's hard to think about something that doesn't exist yet."

"Tell that to Jules Verne. To every science fiction writer who's ever lived."

It's a good point so she nods.

Ernie holds out his arm and says, "Look at this, I've got eczema just like you."

"It's from stress. It will clear up. Mine hasn't bothered me in years."

After April has moved out, Carla says, "Do you mind if I say something about your sister? I think she held you back."

"Held me back? In what way?"

"Kept you from reaching your full potential."

"What potential?"

"Don't be a smart ass."

"Well, if that's true, she won't be able to do it anymore."

Despite Carla's feelings about April, she's the only guest at their courthouse wedding—better to keep it simple, Ernie says, especially at their age. The baby is born three months later. They name the child Todd, after Ernie's father. "He took care of us when my mother jumped ship," he tells Carla. "I want him to be remembered."

April is a doting aunt. She lives only ten minutes away and makes it clear she'll babysit whenever they want. She likes her new place. It has two bedrooms and a decent sized kitchen. She enjoys the process of deciding what to hang on the walls. When she goes to visit Ernie and Carla at the old house, she can see how difficult it is for Carla to make it her own. The fireplace is still the fireplace, the maple kitchen cabinets are the ones they grew up with, and Ernie is reluctant to part with the old green couch.

2019: April 66, Ernie 62, Todd 26

Time seems to pass quickly now. April wonders why that is. Wouldn't it make sense that time would pass more slowly as you age, the way the hours after sunset seem to take longer than the first hours of the day?

She has completed four semesters of French at the college. Since she's over 65, she's given a discount on tuition. She studies hard and has been known to get the highest grade in class on tests. Next year she intends to return to France. Her plan is to spend a week in Lyon and then travel by train to Normandy to visit Mont Saint-Michel. She's heard it described as a mystical island topped by a gravity-defying abbey. You can walk out to it at low tide. When she gets back, she might get a cat. She loved having one when she was a little girl and can't see any reason not to adopt one again.

Ernie and Carla divorced two years ago. Ernie considers it a blessing that it happened after Todd was grown. Todd spent a great deal of time with his Aunt April when he was a teenager. If Ernie and Carla had a fight, he went to his aunt's apartment; she let him stay as long as he liked.

These days Todd is learning how to install and repair HVAC systems. That means April is still the only one in the family who earned a college degree. But so what? Ernie did okay without one. He eventually became head of the maintenance department on campus. Carla now works keeping medical records at the hospital. Ernie had to retire early because he injured his back. He lives in a small apartment and has returned to his old pastime of reading. He's become quite an expert on the history of the Hapsburg Empire, and how its inherent flaws helped create the bloodbath that was World War One. Another subject of interest is climate change. "Remember when I told you about the ice caps?" he says. "I knew about it before most people."

"Yes," she says. "I guess you did."

The town isn't much different than when April was a girl. The college has grown a bit; the lake is still a gathering place for teenagers on summer nights. The auditorium where they saw JFK is still there, although it's been remodeled so it looks nothing like its former self. She has such a clear memory of the day the president visited, especially of the five of them walking up the road. She can picture it all, from how the trees looked, to the expression on her mother's face, to the clothes they wore. Yet because of what happened in Dallas two months later, it is, even more than most memories from her childhood, bittersweet.

In these last few years, April has begun to think about the purpose of life. She's been told that it's about work and family and, if you're a believer, religious faith. She's always found meaning in travel, in seeking out architectural oddities like Mont Saint-Michel and the traboules of Lyon. But can she call that her purpose? Or is it only a hobby? She's unable to say.

Then one day she's driving to the grocery store when a speeding pickup truck runs a stop light and hits her little sedan. She loses consciousness, bleeds profusely, and by the time the am-bulance has arrived she's dead. But something in her, of her, about her, carries on. She no longer has a body, yet she continues to exist.

2074: April 121

Forward through the ether she goes. Others are present. Not ghosts, not souls. Life force? Death force? Let's call it momentum. Soon, some fall behind. Some choose to stop and rest. And a few, like April, carry on. Yes, she has memories: the policeman on horseback, Julie emerging from the lake. If a memory includes an animal it seems better able to persist. Likewise if it includes water or some enigmatic building in France. But the truth is she feels relief when they all begin to disappear. Eventually she consists only of words: cabinet. fiduciary. steeple. plum. She knows now that she is on the way to becoming nothing. It's taken her a long time to get here but it seems right that this is so.

Roberta Allen

Amulet on the Island of Kanum

A man named Marco Polo lived on the island of Kanum. Far from being the reincarnation of the great traveler and adventurer of the 14th century, this Marco Polo left his straw mat only to relieve himself. When the great Marco Polo, who watched him from an impossible distance, could no longer stand the humiliation of knowing this idler had his name, he planted by the outhouse a small pyrite amulet that could easily have been mistaken for gold. Its brilliant metallic sheen aroused the idler's curiosity. As soon as he picked it up, an overpowering urge to travel came over him.

The great Marco Polo was not surprised but everyone else was, including the idler, when he set out in a canoe to explore the many islands he had overheard the villagers talk about. At first, the great Marco Polo was pleased that his namesake had finally "gotten off his ass." But it didn't take long for him to see that the amulet was working *too* well. Even the great Marco Polo could not lessen the amulet's power. He could only track the idler's progress from island to island and hope at some point—in a storm perhaps with high winds and a surging sea— the canoe would capsize. But with each stroke, the idler became more confident, more determined. Trying to console himself, the great Marco Polo thought about his travels in Asia along the Silk Road, the royal court of Kublai Khan, his extensive travels in China. His travels, however, did not console him. What consoled him was the knowledge that even if the idler lived to a ripe old age, he, too, would die and see the world from a place that cannot be imagined.

· · ·

Richard Kostelanetz

Two Single-Sentence Stories

I

When we fired a single shot into the enemy's territory, the enemy fired back, with one bullet destroying the gun that had fired on them; when we fired a volley of bullets, we received a volley twice as large in return; as we moved our canon to the top of the hill, it was immediately hit by a hail of bullets, making its operation impossible; once we sent a patrol of draftees to reconnoiter by night, they were met by a large spotlight that sent them scampering for shade; when we sent a radio signal promising their troops rewards if they surrendered, our message was jammed; when we tried to tunnel under their fortifications, we hit an underground river; once we tossed grenades, they were shot to smithereens before they could land; when we threw spears with poisoned tips, they were met by the force of a powerful magnet that made them all turn left and flow like a herd to a single repository; when we sent up a helicopter by night, it was shot down as it took off, indeed falling into our troop encampment and destroying several tents; when we sent home a radio message proclaiming a victory that vanquished the enemy, the media of the world were supplied with photographs and videotapes conclusively illustrating that we conquered nothing; when we fired a surface-to-air missile, they fired a projectile that intercepted ours in midair, our bomb exploding over the no-man's land between us; when we threatened to use a thermonuclear device that, if our demands were not met by the enemy, would annihilate us all, we discovered that the passkeys essential for detonating our device had suspiciously disappeared; and finally when, demoralized by unending frustration, we offered to surrender and even ran up a white flag, our entreatings were refused.

II

To write an elongated single-sentence story, I find it advisable to begin not with a fully detailed outline with each part in the developing narrative assigned to its appropriate place, but, instead, the nucleus of a motive, such as the desire to explain how such stories might be written, and then to pursue the development of that motive until a narrative rich in nuances slowly appears, the motive thus becoming a kind of scripting machine designed to generate not just the completion of itself but to fill out its fictional scope, much as other artworks of mine depend upon similarly strong ideas that generate imagination as well as restricting it, in addition to creating between those contrary purposes a tension that is itself esthetically generative, all these seeds fueling sufficient energies to make full scale works that represent a surprise to me, their author, who was after all at the beginning familiar only with the procedural idea that could have, theoretically, generated an alternative realization, which is to say that even the story told by me here could have possibly proceeded in another direction to a wholly different outcome; but, the more I think about it, perhaps the most important point to make in this context is that it did not, because it could not, because once I pursued my initial motive, in this case writing within a complex single sentence a narrative about my procedures for writing complex single sentences, the number of stories that could be told were not many but one, only one, which, it should be clear, is what you are reading now.

GEOFFREY PITCHER

May Day

Did walked out the door on a sunny May morning wondering if might just might take the day. Despite the warm blue sky, the threat of shouldn't was looming in the background. It had been a long time since did could, so shouldn't's willful presence came across as a menacing don't. Did was frustrated. Shouldn't had colonized his deep structure to the extent that could, need to, dare to and ought to had long ago receded to the hinterland of can't.

But this was a May Day and with the promise of such, did indulged the possibility of might. Surely will and can would rally to the cause, did mused. Will and can hadn't been in the neighborhood for quite some time now, but did sensed their presence as the May Day sun nourished his hunger for might. With a surge of confidence did blithely strolled past couldn't and ignored mustn't, feeling a sense of daring that even shouldn't wouldn't attempt to repress.

Seeing might at the crossroads up ahead, did hastened his pace. Might didn't know which way to turn: Dare he head north? Could he head south? He used to go west, but since that road was now more travelled, he felt at once trapped where he was and the need to explore new directions. Did savored the opportunity to help might out of his momentary predicament. Movement didn't have to be the only option, did counseled.

Might could enjoy this May Day by mindfully engaging these very crossroads with did.

Might was immediately taken aback by the suggestion. May Day, did? Why, don't you understand, we must be careful and on alert! Did, why would you think that you might when you shouldn't?

SHOULDN'T, howled did! How could you mention shouldn't, might? Don't you know when you simply must? Sometimes when you think you can't you ought to. Man up, might; you can, yes you can, even if you fear shouldn't lingering in the background preparing a don't!

Might paused. To do with did at these very crossroads on this very May Day? Need might will if he shouldn't? Must might ought not? Should might could? Could might should? The options that this May Day was offering began to seem infinite.

And just as might began to settle comfortably into the lap of the May Day sunshine at the crossroads with did, the inevitable shouldn't launched his don't. A most menacing and blustery black cloud hovered over the crossroads and threatened to suck did and might out of their can reverie altogether. The sheer power of shouldn't's don't was enough to quell anyone's must, and might proved no exception. MAY DAY, MAY DAY, he shrieked, running for cover under an adjacent shan't.

Quaking with fear might simply wouldn't accommodate did, and, like so many before, lit out to the west, the hinterland of can't. And as for did, why did was thus done.

Ian Boulton

(eerie music continues; receding footsteps)

Two men crouched down in some sort of . . . erm . . . *foliage.* Both wore green caps with large peaks and their faces were smeared with green and brown gunk. One held a pair of binoculars; the other a complicated rifle.

The subtitle read: (*birdsong, indistinct chatter*)

Dennis was watching the film with the sound muted so as not to disturb Pilar. She had work in the morning and he knew that the films he favoured tended towards the noisy. He liked in particular anything where a previously timid lead character was moved to violence after his wife and daughter were killed in sadistic fashion by a gang of callous youths. Watching the gang members—as ethnically diverse a bunch of cartoon thugs as you could wish for—being taken out one by one by the hero satisfied something in Dennis that he could not quite put his finger on. Equally appealing were those tales of a young woman attacked in the woods and left for dead by a similarly callous gang. Little did they realise that she would recover, train like an Olympian, then return to take them out one by one in elaborate fashion, each death a baroque escalation on the last. The youths in these tales were not so ethnically diverse, most typically falling into a loose redneck category.

On the screen the two men were walking along a jungle path. Despite being fully camouflaged it was easy to spot them making their way between the trees.

The subtitle read: (*birdsong, indistinct chatter*)

From the armrest of his chair . . . always his; let the girls have the comforts of the new plush couch or the old comfy sofa, the battered armchair was forever his, contoured to accept his form and his form only . . . from the armrest of this chair, Dennis took up his phone. In real life, he thought, revenge may be a more complicated matter, come in diverse forms. In real life, callous youths may be unaware that they ever did anything wrong; they may be allowed to grow up and become unsuspecting old men. In real life, the aggrieved may be a little unclear about the motive for taking action, simply have some sense that these people had, say, wasted their time. In real life, the vengeful may not seek instant gratification; they may have the patience of an efficient predator. Dennis's thoughts ran along such lines as he opened the browser on his phone and tapped in the familiar letters, numbers and symbols. He saw a list of topics appear on the screen and he clicked on one titled Sad News.

Here a user known as BigRedMark had posted the following:

Some of you will remember Dennis Sutherland from the Party's days in Hackney and those meetings in the room above the Rams Head. I was thinking we should . . .

Dennis read the rest of the message with satisfaction, enjoying some words . . . *honour* . . . *remembrance* . . . so much that he found himself hugging his knees to his chest. It was all he could do to suppress a squeal of delight. He logged out of the site and replaced his phone back in its holster. He emptied his lungs in a long exhale and a broad smile creased his face. A smile that said: this was so much better than I could have wished for.

On the tv the scene had shifted. A large white house with an impossibly grand lawn appeared, acceptable code for American wealth, safety, comfort and stability. Not for long, Dennis thought, realising he had seen the film before.

The subtitle read: (*birdsong, indistinct chatter*)

Now I acknowledge that you are at something of a disadvantage here because I know the reason for that broad smile on Dennis's face and you don't. Also I know who Pilar is, who else lives in that house, the ages and backgrounds of all these folk and the name of the tiny seaside town where Dennis and the women in his life live. You don't need all this information but it's only fair to give you some of it. So to bring you up to speed without boring you to death let's go back to that day when Dennis felt compelled to feign a brain injury.

Imagine an English cottage. Its stonework. Its leaded windows. Its creeping vine.

Open that impressive oak door with its lion-headed knocker and make your way down the hallway till you get to the kitchen. Here all is bright white surfaces and gleaming chrome. There is an elaborate breakfast bar and at this sit a man and a woman. You already know their names. Imagine how they look. Perhaps you will be proved right.

Watch Dennis swig down the dregs of his tea from a substantial mug that you somehow know only he uses. See him rise to his feet and hear him say: I'll get out of your way then.

One thing you must appreciate and accept, as we watch Dennis leave his home and make his way down to the sea, is just how important the phrase *tucked away* is to him. It lies curled up, nestled snug and deep in his psyche. It brings him great comfort to say it out loud between his gritted Celtic teeth, an accented protection against fierce northern winds that he has never bother to reconstruct. These tones give the two words a nostalgic ring, the sound of a granny pressing a penny in a young palm and whispering *don't tell your Mammy.*

Each morning Dennis sits in his toasty winter dressing gown on his worn old armchair in front of breakfast tv and examines the weather map. He peers at his little corner of the world, that . . . whatsit? . . . *promontory* . . . jutting out there into the sea like a . . . definitely not like a nipple, something that you might be prepared to travel some distance for a brief sighting, that would be remembered once seen, something that you'd miss if it went walkies. No. Jutting out there into the sea like a pimple. Something to be avoided,

ignored if you can manage it, probably be gone by the weekend. Nothing to see here and anyway it's rude to stare.

A rum spot for me to end up, Dennis might whisper to the empty room.

Since moving here Dennis had begun to use, as thoughts primarily, words like 'rum', phrases like 'good egg'. It took him by surprise this campery, this doddery dandyism, but he had decided to embrace it. Each little change between what life used to be back there and what it has become out here was to be welcomed. Why should the new him have the same vocabulary as the old him, he asked himself, as he made his way down the hill from the cottage to the beach (*seagulls screeching, sound of distant waves*). Why think the same? Why dress the same? Why even walk the same? To emphasise this thought he put a little more bantam into his cocky step. 1957, Year Of The Rooster, meet your poster boy. Barrel chest out, undersized bandy legs kick-stepping in their turned up Levis and DMs, Popeye fore-arms pumping, luxuriant grey coxcomb blowing in the fresh sea breeze, a Hokusai wave atop his self-satisfied walnut face. Life . . . this life . . . was good. Tucked away out here.

My commiserations if this was not how you imagined Dennis. But, don't fret, you are spot on with Pilar.

Dennis slowed his step then stopped and turned to face the sea. A cold bright day, the sunlight on the water slick and thick as ice. A lifeboat was on a, presumably, practice run. He listened to the gulls, the erratic yet predictable soundtrack to this fresh start. He let the wind fill his lungs with this new air. It still felt new to him, this health, this well-being, though it had been over two years now since he and Pilar (and Izzy) had made the move here. Over eight years since he cut off all ties with old friends and colleagues. Comrades as were. From time to time Dennis audited himself, checking for regret but found none. Even the tired 'I wish I'd done all this years ago' did not apply to him. Years ago this would simply not have been possible. Years ago he would have had to hate himself for this version of contentment.

He had met Pilar about three years after he had decided to go off the radar. Dennis was lying low, playing dead. Nothing dramatic had happened; he wasn't in hiding as such. There was no big fallout, nothing to look back on and say: so that's why I'm never talking to any one of those fuckers again. That life just sort of fizzled out. At first he stopped making phone calls and sending emails. Then he stopped replying to phone calls and emails. Then he went offline. Then he bought a new phone and changed his number. The old one went out in a black bin bag with some slimy ready meal packs and beyond the pale underpants. Sometimes, even now, he thought of one of the old gang calling him on that phone and *La Marseillaise* pathetically trying to rouse the scavenging birds and rats on the landfill to solidarity and action. Such unlikely reveries (battery life etc.) were pleasing to Dennis. The noble suffering fantasy held particular appeal. Yeah, nothing they can do about it. Didn't want to burden you. Lost on a jungle/icy/watery adventure. Captured by the . . . whoever it was did the capturing these days. Every now and then somebody would try to contact him through Linkedin or something and a message would pop up at his old email address but that petered out after the first year. Then without thinking about it too much he moved out of his terraced house in Whitechapel and into one of his other properties. This was a semi in a part of London so far-flung that few Londoners had heard of it and the people who lived there thought they were in Essex. Nobody who knew him knew about the place. Or his other places. Property is theft and that can carry quite a sentence. Secret property, though, is treason and that can end only in decapitation or permanent exile. Dennis chose the latter. It wasn't planned, as such, not consciously anyway, but if it had been the result of years of underhand scheming

then it couldn't have gone more smoothly. Dennis had gone.

These thoughts came to him every morning as he walked down the hill. Weekdays he would drop off Izzy at school, drive back to the cottage and leave the car in the driveway but not go back into the house. Pilar used the mornings for study and he didn't want to disturb her, banging around the kitchen, watching the horrors of that world far from here unfold on CNN and France 24. No, best just to set off and let the satisfaction with his lot sink in once again.

Don't misunderstand this. The thoughts did not come to him in coherent sentences, rather they arrived in blocky abstract, a collage of feelings, images, codes. They varied a little each day: sometimes a cringeworthy flashback to a meeting above that pub in Hackney or an editorial written for the Party rag would come to him and he would have to dig deep into his inner resources to combat it. But the reassurances were many and they always worked; the shames, resentments and waste lay in wait, IEDs of the subconscious, but now he had the means to defuse each and every one of the nasty buggers. By the time he arrived at the small beachside café for his morning coffee, his mind was a worry-free zone.

The turnover of staff at The Caff was bewildering to Dennis. Always young women, many seemed to work one shift then disappear forever, making it impossible to forge any recognisable acquaintanceship. Today though it was a face he recognised, not exactly a constant but one that made regular reappearances between long inexplicable absences. She was in her early twenties, Dennis guessed, and from China, Malaysia, somewhere out that way. He had no interest in getting to know her, simply wanted an exchange of smiles and a couple of meaningless pleasantries. That imperative to recruit, to see every meeting as an opportunity to enlist a soldier, was long gone. Once upon a time Dennis would have asked her where she was from and either a) dazzled her with his knowledge of her country of origin's political system and the struggles faced by its peoples, or b) asked the sort of probing intelligent questions about the same that allowed her to open up to him, show off a little. But no longer. His evangelical days were over, thank the God he used to talk people out of believing in. His past as a skilled groomer of the disgruntled and dispossessed was exactly where it should be: skulking around that part of his memory that he rarely chose to visit. So this morning he smiled politely after the briefest of hellos and nice days, ordered, paid, collected his full white cup and matching saucer and went to sit at the small table just outside the door. It was too brisk a day for most, smokers excepted, but Dennis liked to look over the beach to the water as part of his morning ritual.

He used this time to bask in satisfaction with the arrangement he had engineered. There was no reflection, simply relish. Dennis had constructed a life in which he had a single simple responsibility: to ensure the comfort of his wife and step-daughter. His only job was to make certain that they felt safe enough to pursue their own interests; that their confidence in things carrying on as they are now was never shaken. In practical terms this had already been achieved. There was no need for Dennis to take an interest in their interests; the best course for him to take was to stay out of their way. He was more than happy to do this. Practice meant he had developed skills in this area of avoidance, near invisibility.

(I know you have a couple of questions, one of which might be where did Dennis get the money to buy his properties? But you have to believe me when I tell you that the answer to that question is not at all interesting and it would be cruel . . . and I'm going to have to ask you to believe me again when I assure you that I don't have a mean bone in my body . . . it would be cruel to make you read it. For now you need to remember that I have chosen this day for a reason. It seems typical but I assure you it is not. On this day . . .

you've guessed it, I know...something happens that crashes this guy's preferred routine. It's coming shortly, I promise. But let's get back to him, drinking his coffee outside The Caff.)

The scene before him was never less than pleasing. Sometimes he would watch early parties of inner city church groups out for a day at the seaside tumble from their community buses, elders barking out the rules of this unfamiliar environment to excited kids. If they were lucky the sun beat down on them but, often as not, the skies were grey and full of a threat that they must have recognised as urban. Other days solitary dog walkers braved the wind and/or rain, flinging tennis balls far along the sand with their cheap plastic catapults. All good for Dennis. But he had a particular affection for days like this day: cold bright and blue, the air almost still but with a bite, the merciless waves quietly pawing at the shore like big cats stalking wounded prey. Just bliss.

Dennis sipped at his americano, looked up at the sky then out to the sea and back again, closed his eyes and imagined the cold sun was warming his wrinkled face. He hadn't yet shaved, nor showered. His tartan shirt was tattered and worn and the fleece he had grabbed that morning for the school run had seen better days. But nobody cared about that around here, he thought. You pottered about in your comfy gear all day then spruced yourself up a bit to pop out at night for tapas and a pint. Who would ever pull you up on a habit that added a little more to the sum of your happiness? Who, in this place, could be bothered . . .

'Matey!'

(*waves lapping, birds cawing*)

Dennis knew not to open his eyes as some recidivistic survival instinct kicked in. Somehow he understood that he must keep the smile fixed on his unshaven, unwashed, face.

Instinct is a curious guide, more sherpa than guru. We want to follow it, know it should be trusted, but when pressed how well can the bastard explain itself? How articulate? How educated? What quality of self-help guide could our instinct cobble together? This new Dennis, though, spent many hours each day without what he used to recognise as a thought. His current version of self mistrusted the glib certainties of his past incarnation, the slick explanations for EVERYTHING that used to come so easily to his lips. He loathed that useless know-all and his circle of jerks as much as he loved the blackbirds and blue tits that lived in his cottage garden. Those birds knew a thing or two. When to venture out, when to fuck off out of it. They knew what to trust. You didn't learn it, you didn't read it, some pillock hadn't told you about it. You just knew.

So it was that Dennis gave himself over to his nature, bought some time, and hatched half a plan before he opened one eye and looked up to see what he knew he was going to see standing over him. The smile was beginning to hurt his cheeks but he made it stay right where it was. In fact, he stretched it a little further. The smile was integral to the success of what was becoming a scheme.

Dennis knew he was going to see a fat fuck with a shaved head standing over him but he was unprepared for quite how much Steve could have let himself go in the eight years since they had worked together. He was enormous. And old. It took an effort of extreme will on Dennis's part to keep the aching smile in place and not to let out a gasp, not of recognition but disgust. Steve wobbled shapelessly above him like a carnival blimp of a bloated mutant Mr Men character. Mr Ravaged Diabetic Trot. He seemed to Dennis to be a perfect visual metaphor for the indulgent waste that had marked both of their first fifty years. Sixty now in Steve's case but, going by the state of him, there were mercifully few to come.

Dennis smiled up at this fuzzy mass, aiming for a look of blank unthreatening fear. Don't hurt me. Everybody around here knows me. I'm no

trouble. The cramp brought on by the rictus grin also brought a film of tears to his empty eyes. That was bound to help the imposture.

'Hello,' Dennis said.

'Matey. Dennis. It's me. Steve.'

'My name is Dennis,' Dennis said.

'I know, mate. It's me. Steve.'

'Steve.' Dennis said.

'Are you OK?'

'Hello, Steve,' Dennis said. 'My name is Dennis.' At this point a tear chose to roll down his aching jawline. He judged it best not to wipe it away and felt it make its long journey down the rivulet created by the smile, around his lips and onto his bristly chin.

'I know, matey. I know you.'

The satisfaction Dennis felt as he watched Steve's planetary face crumble under the recognition that all was not necessarily quite right with his old comrade came as a physical pulse that ran from his toes to his scalp. It was a deep pleasure, a near kin to that first piss on a morning that followed an uninterrupted sleep. Amazing, even that which he dreaded most had turned into pure joy in this place, with this life.

'Hello, Steve,' Dennis said again, then relished the long pause which followed as Steve tried to make up his mind whether to walk away or probe further into what had brought about this sad transformation in this once vibrant enemy of the status quo. In the end it seemed he would have at least a stab at the latter.

'What brings you here?'

'. . .' Smile.

'Are you on your own?'

'. . .' Smile.

'Do. You. Live. Here. Dennis?'

Dennis raised a straight arm, the way Izzy used to do when she pointed towards the outside world but didn't want to take her eyes off the television.

'I live over there,' Dennis said and Steve looked along the beachside street towards a row of beat up residential homes.

'In one of those?'

'. . .' Smile.

Nothing filled the long pause that followed. The role that Dennis played left him no room for manoeuvre or more expressive improvisation. All he could do was prolong the inanity and hope that not-too-eventually Steve would become embarrassed enough not to pry further. And, of course, this bastard would be too selfish to try to help this long lost imbecile by, say, getting him home safely. The longer the pause lasted the more confident Dennis became that Steve would soon wobble off. He had always been a lazy cunt, slow on the uptake, slow to make any move towards an encroaching enemy or the bar, quick to take credit for the ideas and actions of others.

And it was so. Soon enough Dennis became aware that a sweaty fat palm was hovering just over his left shoulder, hinting at a friendly pat goodbye which never came. Instead, Steve drew himself up to his full sphericalness, muttered, 'Look after yourself, matey,' and rolled unsteadily away in the direction of the town harbour.

Dennis did not dare to move until he sensed that he was no longer in sight of the man who didn't know he was his nemesis. When he judged that enough time had elapsed he risked a glance to his left and saw that the danger had passed. He raised a half full coffee cup to his lips, cold now but he drank it down anyway. Needed it. Now that it was over he realised how much the encounter had taken a toll, yet he felt invigorated, adrenalized. And very very pleased with himself. As soon as he was certain he could stand he picked up his cup and saucer and re-entered the café, placed them on the counter. The young Asian girl, busy at the chopping board next to the grill at the back of the shop, turned to him and smiled.

'Thank you,' she said. Sang, really.

'You're welcome,' Dennis said. He half-turned to make his way to the door and was almost out when some impulse, some fresh confidence, inspired him to turn back and talk to her.

'I hope you don't mind my asking but where are you from?' Dennis said.

'Hong Kong.' No attitude. No bristle.

'Lovely place,' Dennis said.

'You've been?'

'Very briefly,' Dennis said though he had never set foot in any part of Asia. 'Vowed to return one day.'

'That's nice.'

'Do you ever go back?' Dennis said.

'No. I can't afford to.'

'No. I can't afford to go back either,' Dennis said.

Why did they both laugh at that? I mean, I know why Dennis was laughing but was it possible that the girl was making her version of the same joke? We'll never know but she was still chuckling when Dennis was in the street and Dennis did not stop shaking his head in wonder at his own wit until he was almost back at the cottage. There, he opened the front door and called out a hi to Pilar whose muffled reply came from the office upstairs. Clearly she was bedded in up there for the day. Dennis walked through to the living room where he spent a couple of hours reading various news sites on his iPad and dozing.

He kept up with the news in a very different way these days. In the UK there were demonstrations against visiting dignitaries from states responsible for appalling and horribly frequent human rights abuses. These were viewed now by Dennis as uncomfortable days out successfully avoided. On the international front reports came in every day of refugees drowning, being sold as slaves, refused entry at safe havens. Awful stuff but nothing that I have to do something about, Dennis thought. He would sign the odd online petition, certainly join in outraged pub talk on the right side of history, but the days when he felt some personal responsibility for the world's waifs, strays and generally fucked-over had gone.

When Pilar called down to him that it was time to pick up Izzy from school she interrupted a complicated reverie about the girl in the café and her admirable openness to answering personal impertinent questions prompted entirely by her appearance. Steve would have a stroke if he'd heard. Steve's wife, the appalling Diane, would stage some sort of lefty intervention.

The way it used to be and the way it is. Up there and down here. Short of being a concentration camp survivor who went on to become a highly paid gigolo, Dennis could imagine no greater pleasing contrast between previous and current circumstances than his own.

That night they paid a teenage girl with elaborate eyebrows twenty quid to keep Izzy company for a few hours. Gemma was the daughter of a woman that Pilar had become friendly with on the university course and was, therefore, trustworthy. Dennis thought she seemed OK, not too sullen, not too fawning. She would let Izzy watch some unsuitable crap on tv and promise not to tell but that didn't bother him and Izzy would tell Pilar anyway.

One of the taxes Dennis paid for his happiness—there weren't many—but one of them was a promise to Pilar to accompany her to see any Spanish-speaking movie shown at the small independent cinema down by the harbour. It seemed to Dennis that these excursions came around with surprising frequency. No sooner had he suffered his way through the ghost story set in an old orphanage outside Madrid than it was time to face the prospect of a bum-numbing tale of some simple Mexican funeral directors. On this night he and Pilar were off to see something from Venezuela. This much he had taken in; he found it best not to listen too closely when

his love read out the synopses from the local free paper or reviews from *The Guardian* online. The less he knew, the less to dread.

In the event Dennis found that he could drift off nicely through this one, the earlier events of the day lending themselves to extended pleasing fantasy. Much more than those on the screen which seemed to concern some poverty-stricken family in Caracas living in a vast crumbling weed-strewn mansion that had been abandoned by its owners. Dennis made no attempt to follow these proceedings. Instead he imagined Steve returning to London and telling his shrill militant wife who he had bumped into today. He imagined the guesswork, what do you think could have happened, then the pity, maybe even some guilt. He imagined the texts to mutual ex-friends and comrades. The phone calls. Emails. The replies, the shock, the regret. The if-we'd-knowns, the so-that's-whys, the jesus-it-makes you-thinks. The head shakes. The sighs. The tears. And maybe even some guilt.

On the screen one of the guys who lived in the dilapidated old house was lying on his back in the ocean, luxuriating in the gentle waves lapping over his body and the sun shining down on his face. Dennis, too, basked. He basked in the satisfaction of the final piece of his reinvention puzzle fixed into place. He basked in what he believed was called closure.

A*nd yet the niggles . . .*

. . . crept up on him. The sense of business unfinished, a satisfaction denied, an opportunity squandered, began to trickle into his thoughts. Like the old days when seizing upon weakness, forcing home your advantage, was second nature to him. Dennis was happy but he wanted that other feeling back, the one that had followed his shock encounter with Steve. This could be the tangy relish that was the refreshing topping to his perfect new life. I handled that brilliantly, ran his thoughts, but I let the scoundrel off too lightly. And I let all the other fuckers off scot free. This moment that he lingered on was not just the stuff of bourgeois nostalgia, Dennis decided. Rather it deserved to be the solid foundation of a grand future structure. A shrine for the ages. He daydreamed about his former comrades filing past this virtual mausoleum to pay their virtual respects to his embalmed body that was not really there lying in state in an imaginary state in a glass coffin that would never exist. The satisfaction that he craved was surely within his grasp. He could taste it. He needed to savour it. He needed to plot. He was not just some aged Scottish warrior eking out his last days on the English coast, he was Lenin in Zurich. He was Trotsky in Coyocoac. Che in Cuba.

'What are you grinning about?' Pilar was crushing a defeated avocado into an almost invisible sliver of grainy toast. Dennis was salting his porridge. Izzy held a crumpet an inch away from her face—butter knife in her other hand—and was smearing Nutella over its surface with forensic intensity.

'A project,' Dennis said. 'I have decided I need a project.'

'This sounds ominous. And boring,' Pilar didn't say. 'Good for you,' she said.

His wife smiled the same lop-sided smile that had beguiled him the evening they had met.

'Just a wee bit of writing,' Dennis said. 'An article maybe.'

That smile. 'Don't show it to me till it's finished. I want to see it in all its glory.'

It felt cruel to Dennis to keep such an angel in the dark but he knew she would not understand his motives. Mischief took up little space in her psyche; revenge even less.

He scooped up the last of his breakfast, stood up from the kitchen table and placed his bowl in the sink. He leant over and kissed Izzy on the cheek, tasting the nutty goo that had landed there in an act of uncontrolled migration.

'I'm just going out for a bit,' Dennis said. 'Clear my head.'

Pilar smiled. This was a pleasing development, potentially. She knew to be wary of her own optimism and normally she would warn herself not to get her hopes up, that this would probably come to nothing. But what if there was a chance that this new project may lead to, say, Dennis fixing some stuff? Or making something useful? It was a bit of a stretch but she could just about see a crude coffee table being something her husband could, after a decent-length course with an exceptional and patient teacher, just about manage to pull off. Or, better, what if the project meant he had to have the odd night away, leaving the cottage just to Izzy and her? What about a whole weekend! But—her mouth straightened—this was no time for idle dreaming. She had an essay to complete and a mound of reading to do.

Dennis stood on the beach with his feet planted wide apart in the sand. He took a deep breath from the wind and his chest pushed out towards the sea. He leant back and looked up at the sky and his sandy hair was blown around his ears and neck. His arms outspread as if to welcome ashore a returning god. Passers-by threw balls into the water for their labradoodles to fetch. Some snuck a peek at the stationary figure, others smiled broadly and tried to catch his attention with a 'Morning!' Dennis was oblivious to them all, an Anthony Gormley study in ostentatious introspection.

Dennis knew himself, knew what drove him, what were his motives. He understood he had never been pure. He had never acted out of malice, not too much anyway, but he was drawn on by something other than principle or belief. It was always the romance for Dennis.

As a boy in Edinburgh he read *Soledad Brother*, *Soul On Ice* and *Blood In Your Eye* and was taken with the idea of the wronged outsider, the revolutionary rather than the revolution. An only child, being fussed over but living on the margins seemed his natural lot. His father worked at the McEwan's brewery as a fork lift truck driver until an accident took his right leg off just below the knee when Dennis was twelve. His mother was a nurse. Both were socialists of the cheery it's-never-going-to-happen-so-dinnae-worry sort. Rocking the boat just carefully enough so as to cause the minimum disturbance was in their make-up. After the accident there was a compensation claim and a redundancy package but his parents were at pains to make sure it was commensurate and proportionate and fair and didn't imply anybody that Dad had worked for was in any way to blame for what could have happened to anybody, even the bosses if they'd been out on the floor that morning. Dennis liked to think he would have made a bit more of a fuss.

In his mid-teens Dennis walked between and around the permanently rain-stained pebble-dashed buildings of Oxgangs wearing a black beret. On his left hand he wore a black leather glove. On the school bag from the Army and Navy Stores he had painted Death To Amerikkka in virulent green. Posters of Tommy Smith and John Carlos raising their fists in Mexico City and Angela Davis and By Any Means Necessary adorned the walls of the bedroom in the family 'hoose', a tiny ground floor flat on a council estate.

Dennis loved The Black Panthers. But . . .

There was something . . .

Something missing. Something about them. Something that didn't quite do it for Dennis.

In later life he would have the same feeling when out on demos about the rights of the oppressed Palestinian people or walking the streets opposing apartheid in South Africa or supporting revolutionary factions in Zimbabwe and Namibia. All wonderfully dreamy causes in their own way but they didn't have the same pull, they just didn't have the romance, he couldn't quite identify with them the way he could identify with the other poster on his wall, the black on red print that offered Dennis everything he desired in a hero. It had the looks, the politics, the martyrdom, the beret. Here was a man that spoke directly to Dennis, a symbol of revolutionary aspiration that surpassed all that dogged Black determination, all that wrongful imprisonment, all that talking and writing and thought. Here was action followed by death followed by cult. Here was Che.

Now at that time Dennis knew less about Guevara than he knew about The Bay City Rollers. But just as all the Islas and Morvas swore eternal devotion to either Woody or Eric, so did Dennis lose his heart to Che. And South America, those countries sticking it to Amerika right on the demon's doorstep. Chile, Nicaragua, the places that lived with the reality of Amerikan interference every day. And—Dennis didn't hide it from himself—they looked more appealing to him. They looked more like him to him. If he'd ever spent any time in the sun, that is.

By the time Dennis was more familiar with his hero's biography he was studying sociology at a polytechnic in East London and living in a squat in a four-storey tenement building in Bow. He was an assiduous joiner-upper, a member of groups both socialistic and anarchic. Stirring—a word the local lefty girls loved to hear him roll around his mouth—was his prime motivator. Getting reactionaries het up, making a noise on the streets, designing offensive banners that begged to be snapped by tabloid photographers. For factions—or any subtlety or nuance—he had little time, but they were hard to avoid. Others found their romance in the futility of the struggle so the smaller and more esoteric the group the more they got off on it. The three members of The Revolutionary Communist Party Of Britain (Marxist Leninist) East London's People Front could not abide their counterparts in other sections of the student communist community, not even their mirror image cell in West London. This presented a challenge to Dennis who shared his squat with this particular faction and was, ostensibly, its fourth member. So he had to be particularly careful when at home to big up Enver Hoxha and not to giggle at the weekly broadcasts from Radio Tirana that all the housemates listened to, let's face it, religiously. For half an hour on a Thursday evening they would huddle round the transistor radio on the kitchen table and listen to statistics detailing Albanian car production, the pros and cons in the eternal argument on the export of tomato puree from the promised land, and the flaws of the approach to state control in other oppressive regimes around the world.

Che and George Jackson it was not. But it was a cheap and convenient place to live so Dennis put up with it and snuck off whenever he could to feed his romantic revolutionary soul elsewhere. Once again it was Spanish-speaking America that came up trumps.

The Neruda Centre in Hoxton became his multi-coloured haven. There could be no greater contrast to the lentil-tinged life led by his flatmates in Bow than the fiery murals on the walls of the community hall, painted in tones unavailable to folk in Oxgangs. He drew the smells of the empanadas being cooked by the refugees just arrived from Chile deep into his lungs; he absorbed the sounds of the folk music being played by world class musicians in exile as if they were Bye Bye Baby or Ride A White Swan; and he swooned at the sight of the women . . . oh, the women . . . .performing the handkerchief dance as if they were back home and the Amerikan-backed Pinochet coup was just some fevered fantasy. After the polytechnic and Bow . . . Hell, after grey drizzly old Edinburgh . . . this felt like life at last.

Dennis often wondered if he'd bumped into the three year old Pilar at that time, traipsing around the place where her parents and their friends gathered to organise. He had asked her, of course, but she had no memory of those early days in the new country. And her parents were long gone.

He thought about it now, standing in the wind on the beach. Thought about the advantage that

working for The Chile Solidarity Campaign gave him all those years later when he and Pilar met on the bleak hinterland between London and Essex, long after the romance of rebellion had disappointed him. Thought, too, about how the timewasters who had strung him along, the architects of his disillusion, could be made to pay. In a small way, nothing drastic. Not actual payback, not really, more a pastime to while away the long days of retirement. Pilar sometimes told him he needed a hobby; well, he almost said, let my pastime be convoluted satisfying deception.

Dennis lowered his arms and faced north then south before deciding on which direction to set off down the sand. He chose north, of course. To the Finland Station.

M oonlight cast shadows—window frame, trees—on the wall above a bed. The sheets appear dishevelled. Somebody's sleep has been disturbed. Probably the woman lying on the lushly carpeted floor in a white nightgown. Well, mostly white. There was a red stain spreading across her chest.

The subtitle read: *(muffled urinating)*

Dennis peered at the action over the top of his glasses, his iPad resting on his lap. He paused the tv and looked down. This needed his full concentration. And the patience that had always been his trademark.

He trawled through the old message boards for a couple of hours, unsurprised to see so many familiar names still arguing the toss about how to explain the loss of basic amenities to the proletariat in the days immediately following the revolution. SellThemTheRope from Leicester was constant in his belief that the workers would understand why their fridges weren't working for a few days or why all travel had been suspended. Dennis knew he had been constant in this belief for over forty years now, resistant to all contrary evidence, and tireless in his mission to belt out all the old tunes till his voice gave out or he keeled over and died.

PartyLikeIts1917 disagreed but didn't care as leaving behind people who didn't deserve utopia had always been his passion. Dennis remembered well the little weasel with his straggly blonde beard and pointy teeth, but can't recall his actual name. No matter. The fact that nothing had changed in that corner of the world where hapless revolutionaries gathered to whine about the wilful ignorance of the working class was all Dennis needed to know.

Heartened, he spent the next couple of nights creating a few fake email addresses and setting up accounts on the two sites he suspected would be most likely to reap rewards. On the fourth night he decided to risk posting a message.

Dennis had no idea if people still use the term 'tech-savvy'—and there's no point asking me; I'm absolutely clueless about these things—but that was what the comrades used to call him and how he still thought of himself. In the early days this meant he could work the camcorder, understand the Xerox machine and more or less laminate a flyer efficiently. Later he became the first of the group to see the potential of the internet in spreading the word to the young proletariat, the first to get a mobile phone. It was Dennis the comrades turned to when their computers went inexplicably dark ('fucking Special Branch') or some new incomprehensible scientific gobbledygook needed translating into good old plain Marxist dialectic. Dennis then was on the ball; Dennis now could still play technological keepy-up with the best of them.

So, as a muscled figure lay paralysed on his bedroom floor, unable to prevent the gang of men in balaclavas from slaughtering his whole family (*distant rustling; cat meaows; ringing telephone*), Dennis opened his laptop and began. The keyboard, he thought, is mightier than the drone.

Making up the names and choosing the avatars was fun. Deciding on where these characters were from, their age, class, the specificity of their political stance: Dennis approached these matters with something resembling glee.

He wasn't afraid of causing suspicion by introducing five or six fresh faces to the struggle; he knew that these wankers would just presume that their message was coming through loud and clear. Dennis played to this vanity plus their need to bolster their ranks, forge new alliances with exactly-the-same-minded strangers, as well as bringing in that rare commodity: the convert. Dennis had insight into the short-sightedness and blind faith of this crowd that was invaluable if his project was to succeed. These people lived in a small world but it was still one that craved a hero. Far now from his Che days, Dennis allied with Brecht on this matter, but he knew he could feed the sad old bastards with the most exquisite epicurean delight of their dreams. A martyr to the cause.

His first intervention came in the form of Granny Gramsci. Dennis decided she was a retired health worker originally from Dundee but now moved down to England's East coast—it was important that this key player lived near the soon-to-be hero. She has a son working with endangered wild cats in South America, a natural step for her boy as his parents had met on the Coffee Brigade in Nicaragua in the 80s. GG is a lifelong, unreconstructed Trot. Her avatar is an image of Supergran with an icepick embedded in her tartan bonnet.

(Perhaps we should take a minute here and acknowledge Pilar's disappointment in this project. Certainly I feel for her but what can I do? Dennis's latest activity took place mostly after she was in bed, seemed little more than a replacement for watching bang bang movies without the bang bangs every night. It offered, from her perspective, no change whatsoever in her husband's routine and, therefore, no opportunities for any adjustments to her own. She lay in bed resenting not just Dennis but also her closest friend Yolanda. Pilar and this dental hygienist came from similar backgrounds and had taken advantage of similar opportunities. Both were in their 40s; both came from the same part of the world; both had found ostensibly undemanding husbands to look after their material needs whilst they got on with their lives. But Yolanda's ancient spouse proved a wiser—well, luckier—choice than Dennis. He played golf and was an active member of the local club but, even better for his wife, he had recently become extremely keen on something called 'walking football'. This activity was designed for geriatrics that simply refuse to give up the ghost that was their athletic prowess. It offered Yolanda not just a couple of evenings a week when the old guy was shuffling around in the floodlights trying to pass the ball to his near-stationary teammates, but also a punishing schedule of away fixtures which entailed weekend travel on a regular basis. There was also a summer tournament in Portugal and a winter trip to Scotland every year till he dropped dead. In all, Pilar calculated, and taking major holidays into account, this meant that Yolanda was free to do as she pleased on some 116 evenings per year. Whilst she remained shackled to a rich man who was deep into playing some kind of video game all night, a so-called 'project' that did not require any movement off the living room couch. For Pilar this was just the latest in a series of cruel injustices, a series that began with the disappearance of several beloved family members for political activities when she was her daughter's age. First that, now this! She could weep.)

O, things have moved on. It felt like we were only gone for a minute but it turns out that weeks have passed! And our lad has been extremely productive. The message boards of the ailing left have been swelled by an unlikely influx of keen new members. They are a remarkably diverse group, too, in terms of age, race, gender and sexual orientation. Scattered around the globe, these new recruits have added some much needed, if you will, *momentum* to the unending debate on the approximate date of the inevitable revolt of the proletariat. Sometimes Dennis would identify an old comrade by his online monicker and have one of his new personae approach them with a question linked to an ex-

isting thread. Other times, he would have the newbies bicker amongst themselves.

Some of his inventions were more, erm, inventive than others. Dennis really tickled himself with StalinWasnaeStallin, another hardline Scottish old-timer who served primarily to give Steve an uncomfortable time. For Steve . . . known online as Steve1956, whether because that was the year of his birth or in celebration of the Soviet invasion of Hungary was not clear . . . for Steve was the target. Steve needed to be reminded of another old Celtic comrade that he may have bumped into at the seaside recently. But the fat bastard was so self-involved that it seemed he was going to need more than a nudge in the right direction. That was the job of GrannyGramsci and StalinWasnaeStallin, good cop, bad cop.

Others, like TopMarx, RedTillDead and TheUrbaneWarrior, kept the conversations from flagging with barely believable anecdotes about their contributions to the cause in Ukraine, California and Dublin. Dennis knew that nobody in his old gang could ever examine these imposters for accuracy or plausibility, their true struggle being an inability to get out of North East London. So his new gang were free to tread these boards like seasoned old hams, starting discussions entitled The Great Global Warming Distraction, The Bourgeois Indulgence of Transexuality and How Can We Turn A Race War Into A Class War? It was all great fun.

But life, as Vladimir Ilyich Ulyanov liked to remind us, cannot be all giggles. Dennis bided his time, waited until his bunch of faux revolutionaries had more substance, more energy, more convincing credentials and back stories, than the tired barely believable flimsy ghouls who had been haunting these pages for decades. It was then that he struck. First he made StalinWasnaeStallin goad Steve into a prolonged and bitter debate over the role that will be played by London in the coming people's uprising. He gave the slob a right pummelling over two whole nights, hammering home the irrelevance to the revolution of Steve's home city. It would remain, SWS argued, a monarchist, capitalist enclave, under siege from the freed working masses of the new socialist republic. This was heartbreaking news to Steve who for over fifty years had lived in the certain hope that the revolution would come to him, not require his enormous arse to shift too much towards it. He took this beating over 48 hours and was a half conscious bloody mess, propped up on the ropes, when Dennis sent in GrannyGramsci on a rescue mission. She brought with her a welcome change of subject. She said, *Steve. You've been around Hackney a long time. You must remember Dennis Sunderland?* Without waiting for the battered wretch to reply, she went on, *I have tragic news, I'm afraid. Poor Dennis finally succumbed to his injuries last week and died in a nursing home quite near me. He was a fine brave comrade and will be sadly missed.* Eventually, Steve came round from his stupor and said, *That's odd. I bumped into him a few months back and I thought something was up. I don't think he recognised me. What happened to him?*

Of all the pleasures of the project, Dennis found the greatest satisfaction in conjuring up his own hero story. The protest, the battle, the injury sustained at the hands of the foot soldiers of the oppressor whilst protecting his more vulnerable comrades, it was just a treat.

(O my dear goodness but this is behaviour is hard for me to take and I'm willing to wager that you are not comfortable with it either. This impulse, this urge, to glorify oneself is incomprehensible to people like me and you, isn't it? It goes against our grain. It's not how we were brought up, is it? It offends our sense of decency, of fairness, of what is right and what is very definitely wrong. But we are not Dennis. And Dennis is a man who is not ashamed to admit that he shed a little tear at his own fictional bravery. Hardly surprising as it is becoming apparent to me that Dennis is not ashamed of anything.)

Following the shock announcement, memories were shared of endless meetings and marches with the bogus martyr. Dennis flinched at the reminder of how bleak it all used to be, mourned the waste that was his old life, but contributed moving tributes to himself, the fallen comrade, from as wide a variety of perspectives as his imagination would allow. As is customary during times of mourning, most thoughts were tinged with affection, all enmities set aside out of respect for Dennis's valiant contribution to their cause. There was, however, one sour note. A poster named LittleRedCook—Dennis recognised him as an annoying twerp who worked in a kebab shop in Dalston—wrote, *Yeah. I remember him. Always seemed to be a bit of a pencil pusher to me. Surprised to hear he became an action hero.*

'Well this cunt,' Dennis said, 'can fuck right off.'

At this point an old faithful companion returned after a long inexplicable absence. Dennis had presumed it abducted or dead, perhaps lost and confused, a demented accidental runaway. But here it came, tail a-waggin', tongue a-lollin', eyes brimming with love. It padded into the room and laid its heavy head on its master's knee. Let's imagine that Dennis is as committed to this metaphor as I am and then you will have no problem believing that he patted the beast's head and said out loud, 'Welcome home. My sense of purpose.'

I n 2029, following a vigorous campaign from dozens of comrades and admirers based on three continents, a seasoned activist from East England known only as Granny Gramsci, was the posthumous recipient of The Dennis Sutherland Award For Solidarity And Sacrifice.

The Grilling

In the hot seat this week we have Dennis Sutherland. A former revolutionary, for thirty five years Dennis plotted the overthrow of the UK monarchy and both Houses of Parliament. At the same time he built up an impressive property portfolio. Retired from both fields now, he lives at the seaside with his wife and step daughter.

What is the trait you most deplore in yourself?

I forgive too readily.

What is the trait you most deplore in others?

Their eagerness to trespass.

What keeps you awake at night?

The usual. Plotting payback.

Have you ever said I love you and not meant it?

Only to a long dead German economist.

What do you most dislike about your appearance?

That it is too easy to recognise me as somebody I used to be.

What's the worst thing that anybody has ever said to you?

We can't just talk about reggae all the time. (You needed to be there for context.)

Which living person do you most despise?

A vacancy for that position has popped up recently, as it happens. I'm scouting around.

Which living person do you most admire?

Modesty forbids.

What is your greatest fear?

Waking up to discover I am Home Secretary.

What's the nearest you've come to death?

Enver Hoxha's *Reflections On China* reached life-threatening levels of tedium.

What would your superpower be?

Seeing through things.

How would you like to be remembered?

As someone who saw through things.

What lessons has life taught you?

People who have the answers have misheard the question.

Tell us a secret

I used to have a brain injury. Years ago.

Paul Kavanagh

The Truthful History of the Conquest of New Ayeléticia

Led Oatllis,
Trans. Larry Caomhánach

I haven't eaten at a McDonald's since I became President. William J. Clinton

If we are to believe Raymond Queneau's[1] theory that there are two plots of land that yield books, The Iliad and The Odyssey, we can safely say that Raymond Queneau's books grew out of the soil of The Odyssey and that Led Oatllis' book was a product of The Iliad. If The Odyssey is the lotus flower inducing hallucinations, The Iliad is red meat. It is the red meat we are interested in, and only the red meat, the red meat might be inferior, but cooked rightly any red meat can achieve greatness. The rest is superfluous, fancy dressing, what we desire, lust for, is the red meat. There is nothing in the world of food that can match a medium raw steak cooked on a grill. The obfuscation, now and again, occasionally, rarely, a book appears that clears away the obfuscation. A book appears that makes you see the world not as a simulacrum but as real. As real as that steak cooked perfectly resting on that plate before you. There are certain books that make the reader feel as if he is stepping out of a boat and placing a foot for the very first time on Byzantium, The Truthful History of the Conquest of New Ayeléticia is such a book, it is simultaneously an explosion and an implosion; it is a bullet through the head; it is a knife in the back; it is a razor zipping across the throat; it is the clicking of the land mine you

have stepped on; it is all these and more, a book that punches you in the face, kicks you in the behind, smashes a bottle over your head. Yes, it is a book of violence. Oatllis is obsessed with violence and the causes of violence, he does not shy away from violence, he welcomes violence with open arms, it is a book, which states concretely that we, you and I, are violent, and I for one concur with Led Oatllis—we are violent, it is a violent book and thank God it is violent because all Conquests are violent. Led Oatllis writes about War and the causes of War, but he transcends the usual War novel, it is more than a War novel, it is a book about Universal Man and his proclivity for War, and this places it next to Homer's The Iliad, places it next to Tolstoi's War and Peace, caught between these books most novels would wither and die, but not Oatllis' book, it stands tall, steadfast, proud, and the gold lettering fulgurates, the words within, on the page coruscate. It is a big book, a thousand and one pages to be precise. It is a difficult book to digest. It is meat and only meat and for some readers too much meat is sickening. Maybe this is why we have bread, onions, tomato, lettuce, Mayo, mustard, ketchup, and a pickle. Little is known of Led Oatllis. Between two Wars, we know, Led Oatllis sat down at a table, in a little hut by the Atlantic Sea, and wrote The Truthful History of the Conquest of New Ayeléticia. He was a soldier; this much is true, it is believed he was killed in battle, as should all good soldiers[2]. Led Oatllis never married. He had no children. Larry Caomhánach in the introduction states that Led Oatllis was married to War, I like this, and that his children were the new recruits that followed him into battle. He was a bellicose man. He enjoyed death and destruction, and once upon a time, this was a virtue. He was a man of stichomythic grunts; he was a heavy drinker, smoker, gambler, lover of meat, when not fighting he wandered through life in a hypnagogic state, he wrote The Truthful History of the Con-

[1] "A Conversation with Raymond Queneau by Georges Charbonnier" (dalkeyarchive.com)

[2] There is a rumor that Led Oatllis had a fatal heart attack sat on his favorite stool in his favorite bar, a result of his diet, cheeseburgers, and Mexican beer.

quest of New Ayelética within an amnion of tequila, cocaine, tobacco, and hamburgers, lots of hamburgers, staring out at an impassive sea. The sea as with the moon as with the sun is impassive to man's destruction as man is, we yawn, we sleep, we wake up and destruction and death continue to unfold, we yawn, we sleep, we wake up. Sometime during the 5 September (it was a Monday) Led Oatllis stood on a land mine. Larry Caomhánach's translation is as masterful as any translation carried out by Barbara Wright, for my money one of the greats. He has captured the brilliance of Led Oatllis and for the first time the English reader is able to read Led Oatllis, for this I clap loudly. He is a truly great writer, as huge and talented as Joyce and Proust and Caomhánach shows this. It is an achievement; it is an achievement as the first translation of the Bible was an achievement. Never before has the English reader been able to enter the dark world of Led Oatllis and I say enter, I shout enter, I scream enter. It is equivalent to the first English reader entering Durante degli Alighieri's Divina Commedia. You are very lucky, very lucky indeed. As you are undoubtedly aware, no translator can capture the true brilliance of an original text, but Larry Caomhánach gets as close to the prose style of Led Oatllis, as close as a bone encircling the marrow. Larry Caomhánach has achieved the impossible and for this, he must be applauded. He is a scholar, and this work will place him between Silvestre de Sacy and Thomas Young, I think.

Chapter One

Carrera and Guyotat are bivouacked on a beach. They are boiling beans in seawater, complaining about travel, about the heat, about the bugs, about the sea, and about the sky, they want to return to Ayelética. Soldiers, hard men, unspoiled by the love of women, they are the first Ayeléticians to visit New Ayelética. The exchanges between Carrera and Guyotat are as masterful, as intricate as the tête-à-têtes shared by Alonso Quijano and Sancho Panza, as laconic and face-tious as those between Vladimir and Estragon, as insightful as those between Falstaff and Hal. Led Oatllis knows Carrera and Guyotat, he has sat with them, smoked, eaten, conversed, he has fought alongside them. By the end of the chapter, we too know the little men that stand behind the giants. It is a masterful stroke. It is a beginning unmatched.

"What's that smell?"

Guyotat laughed.

"No not that kind of smell, I know beans when I smell beans."

Guyotat stopped laughing.

"Do you smell it?"

Guyotat nodded.

"I've never come across that smell before." *Guyotat threw his cigarette away and stood up. He tilted his head and opened his nostrils. He inhaled greedily.*

Finally, Carrera and Guyotat leave the beach and come upon a road. They follow the road and halt before the source of the strong smell. They are the first Ayeléticians to smell and see fast food.

Chapter Two

Back in Ayelética, Carrera and Guyotat stand before the Ayelética Parliament, they are simple soldiers, and so this is a great honor, they are diffident and awed. Ayelética is shown masterfully, with great insight, to be as multifaceted as Victorian London, as beautiful as Rome, as democratic as Athens, it is a place of great learning, sophistication, advancement, Led Oatllis writes about Ayelética as I imagine Romeo would have written of Juliet had Romeo been a poet instead of a street thug, Ayelética is a place unlike any other place, it matches, surpasses Moore's Utopia, Fourier's Place of Harmony, we are blessed, Led Oatllis takes great care to paint the picture, it is one of the longest chapters, filled with Byzantium complexities, with infinitesimal intricacies, even down to the red socks[3],

[3] Only three people were allowed to wear red socks in the empire: the Emperor, the Empress, and the Pope.

but never is it dull. Carrera and Guyotat, genuflecting before the Council of Ayelética, a group of truly wise men, present the Ayelétician Parliament with a sample of the fast food. After tasting the fast food, the Ayelétician Parliament declares that New Ayelética should be colonized.

I saw grown men, violent men, men of mettle and honor faint like maids at the first sight of a grown man's hardened member. I pushed through the stunned throng and saw for myself what had reduced men of power and violence into little girls standing before roadkill.

Chapter Three

To the songs of Al Johnson, the Ayelétician military machine lands on the beach where Carrera and Guyotat had bivouacked and boiled beans. Led Oatllis fastidiously, methodically lists, with the obsession of Homer and his Trojan ships, each military machine, its look, who designed it, and how it is used and the devastation it causes. Led Oatllis's prose fulgurates as he works his way down the page, as Homer glee swelled upon the beach before the great walls. Imagine D Day without the fighting. It is a long chapter dealing with disembarkation. It is here, within the instruments of War, down on the beach, the specks of sand invading the nooks and crannies, that we are introduced to Captain Diadorim.

Never has a man stood before a crowd of men and reduced the crowd of men to insects, to bugs, to larva. Captain Diadorim looked down upon us and knew that we would follow him to the end of the earth; no, we would follow him over the edge of the earth. Never has the sun illuminated so beautiful a paragon of a man. Our awe of this man could only be matched by the awe the moon feels for the sun. We were one hundred moons grasping ravenously at the rays emanating from this bearded sun.

Chapter Four

Following in the footsteps of Led Oatllis the reader is taken on a whirlwind tour of the camp, the reader is taken through a whole encyclopedia of camp life and the machinery of War, it is a place of honor, of anticipation, of men readying for battle, the air is thick with sweat, tobacco, sweet oils, and machinery being polished, tuned, and assembled for War, some men are shown eager for the march, others concerned with life and death, others as impassive to War and the ramifications of War, it is as if they are about to play a game of dice and may in the process squander a few worthless coins. Although Led Oatllis' joy will be matched later in the book, the joy emanating from the ink is palpable, the ink marks upon the page hum and quiver softly, it is pure meat, and pure joy, the ink sizzles like hamburger on the grill.

I perused the camp as though it was a love letter.

Chapter Five

The Ayeléticians capture the fast-food joint[4] that had stirred Carrera and Guyotat off the beach. Whole families waiting for hamburgers and hot dogs are reduced to ashes by the sunguns. The contraption is small mirrors and metallic sponges. The machine absorbs, restructures, and projects the sun's rays. It is a formidable machine, devastating. After the fast food is removed from the fast-food joint, the whole building, everything, even the sign for car parking, is reduced to ash.

"All temples must be reduced to ash so that we can rebuild in our own likeness," said Captain Diadorim.

We cheered and aimed our sunguns at the fast-food joint. As quick as a sneeze it was no more.

For many the first taste of fast food is too much, they go insane, others turn into rabid dogs lustful for more fast food.

At night, under a calm sky, we could hear the screams of those addicted to the bounty. Grown men were reduced to frightened cats under the window, mewling like babies.

Chapter Six

Two hundred miles down the road.

The young woman waits on the side of the road; thumb moves in a small arc when a car tears hissing

---

[4] The Conquest of New Ayelética happened a year before the advent of the first McDonald's.

past. Eyes seek the driver's eyes. Two hundred miles down the road. Head swims, belly tightens, wants crawl over his skin like ants.[5]

The Ayeléticians stop for the lady. Her name is Betty Mellifuliois[6]. She is a cliché, but so what, are Chandler's, Spillane's, Thompson's dolls real, are Joyce's, Proust's, Kafka's women real? Betty Mellifuliois is as real to me as my wife is. Red haired, buxom, coquettish, fiery in temperament and looks, this down on her luck burlesque dancer is introduced to Captain Diadorim.

"Are you from Hollywood?" asked Betty Mellifuliois.

"No," said Captain Diadorim, "Ayeléticia."

Betty Mellifuliois laughed as though she had never heard of Ayeléticia, but the manner in which she recoiled when Captain Diadorim moved towards her she showed us that she had in fact, undoubtedly, heard of Ayeléticia. It is a land where men are men and women are women.

"We want to meet your man," said Captain Diadorim.

"I've had plenty, which one," said Betty Mellifuliois.

"The BIG MAN," said Captain Diadorim.

"He lives in the White House," said Betty Mellifuliois.

"Will you take us there; will you be our guide?" asked Captain Diadorim.

Betty Mellifuliois nodded her pretty, little head in the affirmative for she agreed to be our guide and led us to the White House[7].

With the aid of Betty Mellifuliois, the Ayeléticians set off on the right road to Washington, D.C.

Chapter Seven

The march to the White House is a historiography of violence, lust, mayhem, and obliteration, it is a litany of death and destruction, those possessing weak constitutions should forego the experience, it is tantamount to swimming through

a red river of abandoned fetuses, the pure joy of murder and killing spills out of the ink like blood from undercooked steak.

They aimed their pop guns[8] at us, the popguns went pop, and so we reduced them to ash. Captain Diadorim made it clear as the blue sky over Ayeléticia that no mercy should be shown.

"Any resistance, be it old men, women, child, should be dealt with forcefully."

They had seen nothing as destructive as our weaponry, some dropped to their knees and begged for mercy. It was not a time for prisoners.

Two cops pulled us over. The blue flashing lights perplexed us. We stopped.

They got out of their cop car and walked over. Before they could emit a word, I reduced them to ash. The wind picked up and carried the gray ash away. Seeing as the wind was being helpful, I reduced the cop car to ash, also.

Chapter Eight

Chapter eight is the shortest chapter, but it is still over three hundred pages. A train pulls up. A gang of hobos climbs off the train. The hobos see the trucks piled high with fast food. The hobos run toward the trucks piled high with fast food.

We watched the dog-men, for they were a mixture of dogs and men, they were a slobbering mess, the hair was matted, the clothing lice-infested, the skin weatherbeaten and hemorrhaging, run towards the bounty. It is here that the value of the bounty was crystallized. Before the dog-men could reach the bounty, we turned them into ash. The ash reeked of piss and shit.

Chapter Nine

The Ayeléticians finally reach Washington, D.C. They set up camp insight of the White House and ready for the coming battle.

A dog-man stopped me and asked me if we were planning to stay long. He said he had many friends that were looking for a Hooverville to crash. I reduced him to

---

[5] John Dos Passos. U.S.A. trilogy?

[6] Betty Woodcock, her real name, went on to drive trucks. She married and had six children. She refuted until her deathbed that she was the real Betty Mellifuliois.

[7] There is no Hollywood Romance.

[8] Led Oatllis is being derogatory towards the Tommy gun.

ash and used the ash mixed with water for camouflage. I painted my face and readied for War.

Betty Mellifuliois had been right, God had blessed New Ayeléticia.

Chapter Ten

The capture of the White House is a brilliant piece of subterfuge. Where you would expect a great amount of violence, violence there is hardly any violence, the Ayeléticians simply walk up to the White House and enter.

The President was an old man with three chins and hair that had turned white. He was calm; he was in awe of Captain Diadorim. He listened, nodding his head gingerly as Captain Diadorim told him of our plans.

"Do you agree?" asked Captain Diadorim.

"I would be stupid not to," said the President.

"You would," said Captain Diadorim.

"You'll have to change your name," said the President. "We don't like foreign sounding names."

The deal was struck with a handshake.

Captain Diadorim and the President went to the window, looked out over New Ayeléticia, and dined on hot dogs and hamburgers.

We groaned. The War had ended.

CLIFF SAUNDERS

Lovers on the Outs

I am the wish as crazy as a bed
full of unworn, unwanted jewelry,

and you: You are my fellow
stubborn street refrigerator,

the highlight of my day. You are
awesome in your amused outrage,

your sympathy for doors. You
expect me to wear circus clothes

to your garden of revenge,
but hard times lie ahead for you

and me. Gifted and talented,
you help me translate anguish

into flamboyant music You see
all the pieces of the puzzle. As luck

would have it, I've lost my reading
glasses and can't find a single one.

ANDREW REICHARD

WARD ONE

It was the rising of another grey haze of dawn in the room called Ward One when she said,

When I was little, my parents sat me down and apologized for having me. I remember the two of them sitting on either side, with me in the middle, on the porch of the house my Grand Papa owned, outside of the city. He called it a veranda—Grand Papa and his veranda.

How old were you?

I was little. I'm not sure. Seven or eight.

Not too young. To understand what your parents meant, I mean.

No. Not too young. Well—I understood some things. I could see what was happening, and, in a way, I may have understood it, as a child, better than my parents did. Accepted it, anyway.

As you accept it now?

When she came by the ward, he watched her hands. At first, he'd thought she moved them like a magician's hands about the objects of the room, most of which he couldn't interpret unless he concentrated on them and conjured what they were called. Catheter cables, monitors, syringes. Each time she entered the room, the first thing she did was to sterilize her hands and put on a pair of light blue latex gloves. Each time she exited the room, she removed the gloves and disposed of them and sterilized her hands again. This palindromic sequence she performed silently, flourishingly, as if in an act of prestidigitation upon which he expended long and lethargic contemplation behind a quaking comb of eyelashes.

When she was there he watched her hands without moving. If she did something with her hands that was out of his range of sight, he didn't try to turn his head. He waited. Once, she leaned over him to correct the position of his pillow, and the breast-arch of her blouse nearly brushed against his nose, and he could smell the scent she wore but could not identify it, and he closed his eyes, felt the soft movements of her hands repositioning the pillow behind his head, felt as if he were on a raft drifting upon gentle water.

His dreams flickered along the shoreline of his consciousness in patterns hymenopterous, so that he couldn't tell if they were quickened or delayed interpretations of what had taken place or otherwise what might still take place and hadn't yet.

It was the rising of another grey haze of dawn in the room called Ward One. The breach of his eyelids as gradual. He focused on the door through a slit of sight, waiting for her. When she did not immediately come, he began to panic. There was a button for panicking somewhere in the aura of his reach, and it took him fumbling minutes to remember that he had it bandaged to the inside of his middle finger: a round red button on a doorbell-sized plastic box from which a skin-toned wire tailed out, pressed against his wrist by a second strap, and from there slunk off the bed.

He held his hand above his reclining head and pressed the button with the thumb of the same hand. She appeared.

Is something wrong?

I've woken up—

These were probably the first words they had spoken to each other, but he couldn't be completely sure. She must have spoken to him when he arrived. But he didn't remember arriving—not the space between where he'd left and here, this Ward One; first, presumably, in a list of Wards along a corridor behind his door.

He might have been unconscious when he came—brought: he might have been brought, unconscious. But then how did he know the number of his Ward or have in his memory the image of its sign on the door in separate silver letters?

She must have spoken to him before now, but he didn't remember. What she said now was,

Good. I've brought you food. Can you sit up?
How long have I been here?
Just under 72-hours.
Is this a hospital?
It's a clinic.
What's wrong with me?
You ask a lot of questions, don't you?

Alone, he would have spoken to himself if he hadn't trained himself not to. He would have screamed if it were still in him to scream. In another life. The office building where he'd worked in a low-walled cube, which had not been disagreeable to him, the work, the cube, the long hours of emails with his hands poised on the dusty black keyboard with scraps of poems he'd tacked up for his peripherals and that certain slant of light and those men and beasts of the zodiac, poets from all periods and places the source and substance of which he would have had a hard time explaining to anyone if anyone had asked. And the long hours of ad copy, the shining stratagem of words, which had to be short, had to be simple, simply understood, had to tell them exactly what you wanted them to do and then provide a button—and the hour-long meetings, the meetings through the day and then the drills with the breathing masks, and how they always seemed to—how they came at just the exact most inopportune—and the chicanery of words, watching his hands on the keyboard, typing, sometimes very slowly, very deliberately, tapping out each letter and thinking that letter and reading the screen-width headlines and thinking about them, the words that made them up and what they meant—and these copied, pasted, cutout, tacked up scraps of old words next to the copy on his screen where—were anyone ever to have asked—he might have pointed out the difference between guile and guilelessness, or else the difference between meaning and senselessness, or else—but then the lines that were just a part of that place where he spent so much of his time, while the headlines—

Now, you know that button is for emergencies—yes, that one, strapped to your hand. For emergencies only. I thought something was wrong.

There are things I don't remember. Blank spaces. For instance: I can't recall how I got here.

You were brought in with a pick-up crew. They found you in the streets, no identification.

Am I sick?

Yes.

I know I'm in Ward One. I can picture the outside of the door with the label. Why is that?

Within the first hour, you tried to leave.

I wasn't allowed to leave?

You're sick. A sedative was administered.

That's why I can't move my legs?

Your condition is worsening.

I'm afraid.

Of what?

Of sickness. If I stay here I'll only continue being sick. If I go out into the city, I'll die. I'm afraid of sickness and of staying here, but also of a death like what would happen if I were to go— I'd always imagined that I'd die in a way that—I thought I'd have time to reflect on what I'd be leaving behind, what would outlast me. I never imagined the—the end of the—well, of the world, to feel like— an end.

A conclusion—

It's just that I'd always imagined myself dying in a way that—where I was the only thing dying is what I'd imagined. What I mean to say is, I thought I'd be leaving behind—

> Before she left the room, she removed her blue latex gloves and sterilized her hands with the sanitizing gel from the dispenser on the wall by the door, rubbing the substance into her hands and making circular grasping gestures—one hand grasping through the tunnel that the other made, fingers coming through closed and then opening, grasping, and then turning and sweeping over the back of the other and making a tunnel for it to grasp through and then repeating to make a winding and highly—he thought—contemplative pattern.
>
> When she had gone, he lay in semi-dark under an off-white blanket pulled up to just below his shoulders. Just like that, he slept. He woke to the sound of a bird killing itself suddenly against the surface of the window,
>
> but then he thought he might have dreamed this;
>
> and, after all, it could also have been that someone had thrown a rock. A thrown rock, or some object, against the surface of his window, not hard enough to break it, but enough to wake him up. If it happened again, he'd press the button, he decided, deciding he'd panic. Call her in and have her see what was happening out there and make it—better.
>
> This realization—that he had complete and childlike trust in her, his nurse whom he didn't know—startled him a little, this attachment. And it might only have been that he was dying, but, of course, there was nothing she could do. It was only that he didn't like the thought of being alone.

Is something wrong?

Yes, something is terribly—

> She came in and stood by the edge of his bed, and she'd forgotten to sterilize her hands or put on a pair of blue gloves. Or possibly she hadn't forgotten. White, small hands, held at her sides. He watched her from the bed, not moving, waiting for her to be angry with him for pressing the panic button again after she had explicitly said—
>
> But instead she said,

When I was little, my parents...

She said,

It was my Grand Papa who told me stories about what we used to have. By we, I mean people, generally. He used to read to me from a leather-bound book with diaphanous pages.
I think I know the one you're talking about.
He read to me from his rocking chair on the veranda, when I was little. I have one particular memory of him doing this during a rainstorm. Sheets coming straight down from a beige sky that had sunlight behind it, sunlight over the city. Rain you could still—
I have a memory like that too. Raining, maybe gentler than your rain, maybe a drizzle. A bird or two in the trees. I used to know which bird was which by the sounds they made, you know. Without seeing them, I mean.

> He asked her if she blamed them, her parents, and she asked for what, and he asked if she blamed them for having her or if she blamed them for telling her they were sorry for having her, either one. For an interval that seemed to encompass the motion of the sun through the vertical blinds over portions of the window, she remained silent, looking at the window, but, he thought, not through it. Her hands were still on the sleeves of her blouse, her arms crossed below her breasts, and she seemed a complete person. He was aware of thinking that: her self so complete in his vision, so still, as to seem like the portrait of a Dutch painter, the far corner of the room dark behind her and bare. To save himself from her silence, he asked again,

Do you blame them?
When I'm being ungracious, I do blame them.
Honest of you.
But blame is just an idea.
So are a lot of things. Are ideas, I mean.

> He looked around the room for an idea, but nothing presented itself. His eyes settled again to her hands where they were folded in her lap while she talked to him, this time seated in a wire-frame chair that she'd pulled up to the side of his bed. Her eyes, in every light, were so incessantly grey that he wondered what other colors she could possibly see. He tended to avoid them, but had also no reason to distrust them. In fact, it seemed graceless of her to be so open with him.

I assume that, since you're talking to me so much, it means there's nothing, really, you can do.

And, also, apprehensively,

How long do you suppose I have?

> In his dreams, saw his hands as through a ray of electromagnetic radiation, as though the act of his vision were performing this feat of transparency. The best way to describe the diffracted flesh around the bones of his hands involved talk of ghosts. He spread his fingers, each finger adjusting separately, flexing—and there was a certain amount of electric pain.

If this were a hospital, there would be a television on the wall across from my bed, I suppose.
Then I suppose it's not a hospital—

> It was the rising of another grey haze of dawn in the room called Ward One where outside the world— The word *departing* done across his vision in good gothic print,

and he could picture these things about his life, but only with a great tightening of concentration or else an equal loosening of dreams. He had very few images left to him that weren't these images here, in his last waking hours.

He hadn't slept because his legs, which had been waking up, had kept him from sleeping—the tingling, almost painful sensation under the sheets.

In the night, he'd removed the strap that held the panic button to his hand and then let the button down to the floor by its chord, and now he lay on his back, working his hands clenched and unclenched to keep himself from screaming. Slowly, he brought his knees up in a little mound, and he gripped his ankles with his hands and pinched the skin there until it began to hurt, which he took as a good sign.

Standing up took the remainder of the morning and an unspeakable number of minor interludes.

Beneath his gown, an uncomfortable allotment of cables, and also intravenous tubes, many of which were attached to the IV stand that he wheeled entire to the handicap-width door and, there, pressed the button for the automation of its inward swing. On the door's outer surface: Ward One in silver serif letters.

> And in dreams were the iridescent blue barn swallows that flew out of his childhood from the eaves of a fog-floating veranda with beyond the blank windows; and, certainly, he'd like to believe not just that all was God's will, but that God's will was good: it's ultimate end; it's—ultimate end. The sadness of all that was passing away, incorporated, as it were, into that—whatever it was that was coming in a-wing on the colorless silver skies where before he used to see the iridescent—

Were you ever sorry for yourself—for being in this world—yourself?

> They might have been the last two left. But no. How ridiculous to think so. That this could be one of those stories, and him in it. He was dying. Could barely get out of bed. There was nothing even she could do for him now but make him a little more comfortable, and if he asked himself why she was doing even this—
>
> He was aware of himself thinking of her hands and wanting to hold them, her hands. Perhaps just one of them. He might ask her if he could hold one of her hands for just a minute. But he imagined her neglecting to remove those blue latex gloves, and so he said,

But you have to wonder why your parents didn't just tell you it was going to turn out all right, I mean—

You mean lie to me?

Of course, lie to you. What else?

What they did is what else.

You said you blamed them.

Only when I'm being ungracious, which is less and less often, now.

Well, I'm glad you seem to be feeling gracious right now because I think I need—yes, the pillow just a little—

Sometimes, I almost think that they were wise, preparing me the way they did, allowing me to become detached from them at an early age, so that when I didn't have them anymore—

God shield us from wisdom then. I say that because it sounds like your parents were too wise for their own good. For your own good.

Is that your way of saying ignorance is bliss?

No, of course not. Not ignorance and not—no, of course not! What I mean is—it's a prayer, for protection against our own wisdom—what led your parents to wish they never had you and to tell you this, because of what they knew.

Not wisdom either, then. Knowledge.

Yes, knowledge is what I mean. It must all be erased—all our trying to make sense of—all our own words, I suppose, before we can begin to—

Begin to what?

He looked around the room for help, but nothing presented itself. Not here. Not in this cold clinic, this place of patient procrastination. Finally, and in near desperation, he said,

Begin to end.

Now he stood in the low-lit hallway with his hand on the trunk of his IV stand. Doors receding down a corridor. Of course. One far light flickering on the edge of death. Of course.

But he wasn't finished. He told himself this, silently. He wasn't finished. Commanding himself, silently, and maybe mouthing the words a little— commanding himself to believe not just that all was God's will, but that God's will was good, it's ultimate end, its conclusion.

They'd taken his clothes, and so he stepped forward in an unfortunate hospital gown the color of creeping phlox, and there was a small squeak in one of the wheels of the stand, and there was the drip bag by his head with its liquid sloshing. He became aware of a problem and stopped. The door he'd just passed read in silver serif letters: Ward One. Looking back, he checked his progress from his own room whose door still stood open, and then he reminded himself that he was sick and that it was too late for explanations of form. Far too late; though, he did consider calling for her.

But when he arrived before the third door, he confirmed for himself a pattern.

While you're here, might I point out the difference between sense and senselessness? It might seem obvious, but—

I've brought you a yogurt snack for lunch.

Don't you have anything more—substantial?

I'm afraid supplies are running low, food included. They're not bringing anyone else in. The clean up teams have stopped returning, and we are on lockdown. What were you saying about—?

I think I might panic. It makes some sense to panic just now. It seems that I am unable to die without—that cough: are you sick too?

You're the patient. We're worrying about you right now.

But—are you running this place alone? This clinic. Helping patients alone, and—how can you be doing this by yourself right now with the city, I mean everything, the whole, God—the whole world? Where do you find the strength, when even your body—

—dreamt her in a Dutch painting, with her white hands folded, one over of the other, on the back of a blue armchair and her face in that dishwater shadow through which the grey of her somber—her eyes beheld him and were grey and were patient in the painting that she was and her terrible, her sad patience.

After treading past another number of doors, he chose one when he decided he could go no further and opened it. And went in to Ward One where she sat in a wireframe chair telling him that when she was little her parents sat her down and apologized for the world, for the simplicity of its undoing, for not being, themselves, God.

And when it was time for her to leave, she stood by the door and by himself standing there still, and she removed her pair of blue latex gloves, turning them inside out and one by one as she removed them and depositing them in the receptacle by her feet and then sanitizing her hands with the foam sanitizer attached to the wall above the receptacle before which she stood, rubbing the substance into her white hands by rotating her wrists and overlapping her hands with her hands and all the while watching him where he stood close to her in the doorway and saying nothing.

Alone in his apartment at night during curfew he would occasionally weep, but not at work like some of his peers when outside their windows the men in white robes repeating words from either Revelation or Genesis: *And the Lord regretted that he had made man on the earth, and it grieved him to his heart.* And the coy despair in a midnight-shaded paint sprayed along the terminal wall that read, Blessed are the ants, for they shall inherit the Earth; and the riots and those—that pair of black two-inch heels abandoned on the sidewalk that he'd had to swerve his bike to keep from hitting, though he hadn't been able to look at them directly, which seemed to be true about a lot of things these—including the headlines, those that were still running, still screaming, still printing or printing again after the crash that had finished what work he'd still had and had him pedaling over the streets with his issued mask around his neck in case the sirens came, even though no one knew if they worked, the masks, or what they were supposed to keep out, keep us safe, Father, from uncommunicative corpses, and nowhere in this city to show one's exhaustion, nowhere. And he might have read the words in print that slapped like a dead leaf one day against the palm of his hand when he held it up for a shield in the wind, but for the absence of details and how they, the words, occurred not so much as words written and, thus, read, but more like an idea that had simply occurred to his mind—the guilelessness of a gothic fragment that was just a statement without a story, and the finality of those words, the uselessness of any words to follow—the perfect truth of them that created a, a poetry, he thought—the poetry of the—which was to say the complete lack of ulterior, political, persuasive—the fact of the journalist's observation, and the way he or she must have simply looked out a window at that certainly slanted light and immediately printed what he or she had written without another backward thought or a backward—written simply, *The World Is Now Departing From Us*, and

END

S.T. Brant

Three Poems

The Epitome Point
(Transtromer IX)

i. Compass Planes

Denseness built around denseness : compound
        ephemerality of the translation :: Away
from the most conscious point : the unconscious point ::
        Life battling's career : in cards the lower hand ::
Transcription of a time concealed : lost guises lost
        in movementless existence decoupling ::
Undirected : : Un.

ii. Up to the Light

Chthonic overwhelming residue : surmounts the throne of :
        within : eddying reincarnations ::
Voyage into dark : inescapable ship & shipmates :
        Time's dualistic bite : chromomaniac sins ::
Diminuendo of Memory : true past eves :
        lost from : gigantic whole ::
Time's resurrection in the conscience : field envisaged :
        beyond : matter parabolic ::
All : free beyond the field : unmove : unsound : unthought : :
    Un.

iii. Nucleic Harp

Salvific landing : the Up descending ::
        Gravityless sounds : resound perogatives unwhim ::
Wrath indignant : from above ::
        Salvation's patience replies : :
Un.

God & the Natural Particles of a Timed Divinity
(Transtromer X)

:: Life : tumored mass :: logical hours' perversion : abdomen of time :: how long :
  black limbs black : & diurnal :: ::

:: Subterranean basal life : utter height :: passing by of : Fate :: into :
  other seasons : other hands :: ::

:: Night : crushing curtain :: high decay : light :: unstoppable fluttering :
  atoms in : the still :: ::

:: Calcitrant violet : form of Lord's shadow : of one's self seen ::
  caustic palpability : world's eaten : nucleus ::

:: Breath within : overpowers : lungs that twist : breath within ::
  rebeginning : reasserted form : old souls ::

:: Transects the cross of Time : God :: ghost through : oblivion of body ::
  god immune : cargoed transigence ;: of : cargoed souls ::

:: God speaks in chips of light ::

Capitalist Triptych

I. Abandon All Hope

Sitting at his desk in his classroom while his students are at their desks talking with each other, their assigned work put aside, the internet having crashed throughout the entire school district on the first day back after winter break, he deludes himself at his computer that this semester will be different, that this whole year, not only professionally, in which he's miserable, but aesthetically, the style of living he thinks worth living, will be different.

II. Stalled at the Desk of Life

The ocean of hours in this minute . . . the years that have passed between 8 am and 8:01... O the rusting consciousness in him that's chained to the gate of Life, looking out at the lilacs where the Living frolic and he, behind the bars where the living watch all that they should be but have failed to be up to now and have little optimism to become. Being dies before brain death banally calls.

III. Thinking of a Job You Want Working at Job You Hate

The Possible Canal has roped the walk off. Chains restrict the passage to the gondolas, and the gondolas not yet burning are being moved toward by the gasmen with their canisters. To burn the vehicles that travel upward to all the possibilities yet accomplished, to limit the world to the already happened and tell the passengers waiting around the fires, heartbroken, quizzical, to be content, that this is how it is and how it should be and all is right. We accept this proclamation and move away.

David Ossman

From PIECES FOR SPEAKERS

Manures

I. Digestion and its products

let us suppose
that we have a full-grown ox
which is not increasing in any of its parts
but only consumes food to keep up his respiration
and to supply
the natural
wastes
of his
body

When food is given to animals
it is not *put out of existence*
but is merely *changed in form*

II. Dead Animals

If a dead horse be cut in pieces
and mixed with ten loads of muck
the whole mass
will in a single season become
a valuable compost

Small animals
such as dogs, cats, etc.
may be with advantage
buried by the roots of grapevines

III. Evaporation

when they have lain for some time in mild weather
grey streaks of *ashes*

having been *burned* away
nothing but the ash remains

this is called *fire-fanging*

IV. Hog Manure

Hog manure is very valuable
but it must be used with care

very liable
to make cabbages *clump-footed*

to induce a disease in turnips
called *anbury*
(or fingers and toes)

it is so violent in its action

v. Green Crops

ammoniacal liquor of gas-houses
soaper's wastes
bleacher's lye
lees of oil casks

which we have not space to consider at length

vi. Sawdust and Soot

A handful of soot
thrown over a melon vine

vii. Mineral Manures

while the ash of *potatoes* contains more of *potash*
than anything else

viii. Recapitulation

THE OX makes poor dung and rich urine*
THE HORSE makes rich dung and poor urine*

*comparatively

ix. Night Soil

The *best* manure
within the reach of the farmer
is *night-soil*

The color and odor
of the rose are made richer
and more delicate
by the use of the most offensive
night-soil

This wonderful change of *night-soil*

Mix with it a little charcoal dust
prepared much
dry earth

what is called poudrette

This mode of doing this
must depend on *circumstances*

Household Discoveries

I. THE DAY'S ROUTINE

1. To Quicken Low Fires

When a coal fire burns low
throw a tablespoon of salt on the coals
put in an old ham
or shoulder bone
or use
old corks and empty spools

2. Care of Stoves

By a daily brushing or rubbing
and by a thorough blacking
and polishing
once a week

Remove cinders and ashes each morning
brush out the firebox and flues
brush off the outside
with wings
or a hair brush
blacken
and polish

Rub lard under the fingernails

3. Stove Blacking

Beat up the whites of 3 eggs and mix
in ½ pound of black lead
dilute with sour beer
to the consistency of cream
boil gently for 15 or 20 minutes

4. Nature of Dreams

Many persons
attach more importance to dreams
than is either wise
or proper

II. HAIRDRESSING BOTH FOR MEN AND WOMEN

1. Razor Strops

Comparatively
few persons
seem to understand
the theory
of stropping a razor

A good razor stop
may be made at home by
anyone having a little ingenuity
which will give at least as good satisfaction
as the purchased article

The snuffings of candle wicks
in place of the emory
are also recommended

2. Red Hair Dye

To darken red hair mix 1 dram each
oil of nutmeg and rosemary
1 ounce castor oil
2 drams cantharides
8 ounces French brandy

work a teaspoon or more
into the hair each day
with a moderately stiff brush

3. Baldness

Or cut a small onion in half
and rub the scalp with it
just before retiring

rinse well
with soft water
and castile soap
in the morning

III. COMMONPLACE BOOK

1. Night Air

If we do not breathe
night air at night
pray what shall we breathe?

2. Artificial Illumination

Artificial light
is the third most important
of the necessaries of civilization
after the items of
clothing
and shelter

3. Weights and Measures

The common measure of value
is money

IV. TO SILENCE NOISY SCISSORS

When one has much cutting to do
the constant squeeking

correct this by breathing
into the open hinge

after which open and close the scissors several times

Jace Lee

Four Dream Poems and One Sign

dream poem

i saw this poem in a dream last night. i had all the words when i woke up: crisp black serif font on aged paper, author and year published. as soon as i woke up i was supposed to write it down. it was short- just 2 or 3 lines, all across the page, no line breaks. i forgot lines 2 and 3 first, and then i tried to recall the author, even just a part of the name, and then i forgot the first line, but if you asked me i think i could still tell you the cadence: Du-dun dun du-du-dun du-dun du-dun.

3/31/2022 8:27am

this morning the asphalt i drive on
looks new because it is black
because it is wet because
it has rained overnight but the sun
is out on my drive and i
saw a black bird, flying erratic
in front of an orthodox church
with copper green domes but then
no, it's just a plastic bag but then, a bag is
a function and plastic is the flesh,
a bird is a function and flesh is
the flesh, no
A flash of light stayed on the road
waving back and forth, a sign from
god, I saw many today.

6/10/22

pre-cognition a rush:
i think i taste a floorplan of you
before, i think i've been in this room
Before
trade speed for margins which
rest differently on my tongue
in another dream, in which you were you but different,
there was a poolhouse i was trying to leave in

equal parts, one of many
men, polite and towing
still-unfamiliar things, well,
in this picture. i left before
the boats made it to the water. i watched
a white dog for a while. the white dog
was in front of a bush that was in
a sterile garden, but
that is the picture. with my elbow
in the car window i'm with you.
i'm tapping out a dream on the door.
i'm waiting in the lot to dream.

7/20/22 DREAM HOUSE

Theres this courtyard
I keep seeing
Its you
Around the corner
Of two beautiful
Limewashed
Walls
And lovely floors
And lovely rooms
All around
With generous
Bathtubs and
Finely aged
Coatracks and
Damp towels that have
Drunk you in
And old chests
And soft sun
And grooved stone
And our feet on them
And our mothers feet on them
And white cloth on the windows
And these walls eating us so well

7/24/2022

in which
i watch
blood pour from your chest
so sudden
like you'd reached and
opened a spout
that's neither here nor
there, no thing
spatial and then
we moved on to better things, like
if we were in that hallway we thought
we'd forgotten
like if we saw a beast on the rooftop
had to tear into us, had to
learn teeth on bone like
if we were a fishtank
in a moving ar if
we were facing so many
doors none opening inward
if we noticed
for the first time the
ceiling was offering
us sweetness

Vivian Ia

Three Poems

orphan songchild
magnanimous

on earth he was always elsewhere silkening
sadness, always there
for others'
down-
ward
turns of tragedy,
made due on potent small times,
spun secret heartstrings
in loving
every
drop
of spilled milk,
there having been
no mother's

a bountiful
sop-
up,
little pariah boy,
the bounty is a sop-up

you just wait & see
the returns your rejection
drums up

worm moon

between
pollen & snow

winter did,
in deepest rime,
end with a whimper

new, restless childborn breath
what rhymes with

the barely beating heart
of a frozen pond?

between pollen
& snow,

could harken

could happen

terminal delirium

once civilization stops running on oil
there will be no more need for coffee

future elixir
in ultramarine please

*

not that the gutter's gold shone
any less than the mine's shined,

the next time they do civilization
may it be easier on the eye

Matt Morris

Two Poems

Stalin's Fingers

to churchill they were
horrific symbols
each representing
a million dead souls
lost in the famine

a wild estimate
based on a banal
gesture it could have
meant anything per-
haps stalin was just

showing off his jazz
hands synchronized to
music that an old
stick-up-his-ass bull-
dog couldn't hear &

wouldn't understand
if he did maybe
he wasn't listening
to churchill at all
but was looking for

dirt under his nails
or hangnails also
it bears mentioning
that he might have been
simply waving off

the server heading
their way to ask them
about dessert what
if stalin widely
known to suffer bouts

of depression held
up both hands to say
stop stop let's not talk

about such sad stuff
today then clutching

his hat to his heart
he said why not ask

me about my hair
instead tell the truth
doesn't it look great

history shows it was
thick black & wavy
like a cool night breeze
rustling through wheatfields
of the collectives

on the russian steppes

to Michael Parenti

3 in the Morning

I don't know what I'm looking for but I'll know when I see it
ruled the supreme court a documentary maybe a secret
society that once buried spanish doubloons all over

the americas in an intricate enigmatic
series of interconnecting underground tunnels if not
an infomercial master chef raising a racket about

his amazing stainless steel wok big 10 log-rolling tourney
replay black & white quiz shows misnomered sitcoms their glassy-
eyed stars dead or else zombies an airplane crash in washington

makes the news as do war famine pestilence propaganda
for mass consumption on channel 19 a raw depiction
of the daily lives of an average working class family

made with the same stringent eye for detail that you might expect
from the flintstones now burns into my brain for eternity
flipping as if I'm watching history rewind until I've

gone full circle back to the beginning back to channel 2
where experts agree it seems quite likely creatures from a vast
unknown underworld city were somehow bioengineered

for the sole purpose of guarding the gold a crazy theory
you have to admit but one that explains the swastika
used to mark the spot on the hand-drawn map saying to dig here

David Wolf

Two Poems

When I Was Little

When I was little,
when the toast popped out of the toaster I would say, "Toast pop!"
Now I'm not so little. Too much toast.
I'll continue by saying I feel fragmented as ever,
still at sea in body and soul, fairly sure that October will arrive in the hours to come,
puzzled most days as the city birds are about the overcoats that color the world
of the fortunate and not-so fortunate,
well aware that . . . duly noted.
Let's move on like a new wave forming beyond the horizon, when and where least
    noticed.
I'm still in training for the unexpected, the unanticipated,
the sub-zero or the flaming wind-up to universal becoming O Time, listen as we sing
    and ask
once more, little lamb, who made thee? Dost thou know who made thee?
as the almond wind of memory circles the chafed monuments of epic plunder
and mad, cruel erasure.
Sometimes you feel like an adjectival nut, sometimes you don't.
Babble B-ball Bible Bobble Bubble . . . what a difference a vowel makes.
Some might say this poem is a joke
but I would disagree.
No, it's a poem (more on this later),
and life is a joke told by the big comedian who is not just here all week
but here for eternity,
or isn't, which could be the best joke of all.
When I was little I chose as my joke for trick-or-treat
(in Des Moines, Iowa, you have to tell a joke at each house when you go trick-or-
    treating)
I chose for my joke the following: Who invented spaghetti?
A man who really used his noodle.
When I was little I had some growing up to do.
Still true.

Ours Is Not to Idle By

Ours is not to idle by.
Ours is but to pierce the lie.
So let's try it again with another work of art.
An easy lie for starters: the water you see in magazines is fake, it's paper water,
peripheral to the history of trust
and the expiration date of your latest narrative currently on pause.
In the same spirit, I took the day off work to visit the zoo and hang out
with some different animals.
It was autumn, the cicadas were singing to the lucky pigeons.
Let the insults pass, I thought, let them climb in and out the transom of mid-
    afternoon memories.
The tickets are made of impure air.
Someone is singing in Atlanta, don't you think?
Success can be an abusive concept, and it's kind of funny when you break it down
to its two syllables: Suck Cess.
Language is full of such unintended humor.
Take it easy
as pain lifts knowledge's wallet once more.
The big subscription is running out; the renewal offers are fewer and far between.
O, *Elle*, let me leaf through your semi-autonomous anesthesia,
so vigorous on the eye, sing *cuccu!*
Look up, around, back, forward if you can take the time, the seasonal smooches
    turning to pecks.
Winter, I love you still, trying as you can sometimes be with your defensive weather,
but vows are vows.
Here's what the justice of the peace said at my leisurely wedding:
"Repeat after me, though if you are uncomfortable repeating after me, you can pass."
That wasn't my real wedding, rather just a performance work.
Like time itself, which someone said was a river, but it's really merely time, which is
    just an idea,
but a heavy one, no f-ing shit.
The months stream on, and I think I'm going to faint.
On the drive to work the other day, I noticed someone had changed the sign
"Skunk River" to "River Charon."
I would like to think that was a high school prank executed
by some AP English kids.
Anyway, all my bats are in a row, hanging like teardrops in need of a shave,
dreaming of the stars firing down on menacing ducks spitting interest-charge fine
    print
over the phone, and while I wait to have my real concerns addressed, I think
when I grow up I want to be a lay sage, hedging.my remarks
in torn relief at the foot of obscure monuments, peopled by chafed heroes,
wondering about the stone underwear under all the pomp.

Timothy Dodd

Two Poems

Late Evening Interior, With Three Lamps

Vuillard sips my Glengettie
on the aquamarine of parlor

missing secrets, a keeper, tea
cup chimes darkness in century

old shade. Pour the tone to me
and have you watched a fish,

he asks, darting flat-eyed amidst
sycamores. A staring bio, no,

as retinas fall to sills, bandaged
with drapes seeping like sap

from socket. Smiles mirrored
by crossed legs slanting the floor,

maroon carpet, blood velour
with a little cream. Cherrywood

dressers are sweet tobacco sky,
appearing not outside, but over

the mantle. To your wine bottle
holding more in its emptiness,

a crooked face where eyes stir
the bright yellow behind talk

in lamps and pipes. Violin is bread,
someone here, otherwise common

place. It is sight for color in tight,
cornea ridden, diseased, but beauty

streams through rust, blind. That is
not a fairy woman at the window, sir.

A Range of Misconceptions

    A bore bears down
    his manhole leading
    to a tank of chirping
    finches, tiny-taloned
    translucence, pinked
    in grainhunt. Spills,
    she says. No pattern.

    The pattern is death:
    hats off, clip it and die.
    We can't impregnate
    whales without instinct,
    rig bats to blasphemy.
    If you noticed, a tree
    will grow right through
    your earlobe, Antietam.
    It's up to you to move.

D. A. Hosek

Two Poems

These Ten Thousand Nights

In these ten thousand nights I've spent alone
I've never lost sight of your face,
       Never sought other comforts.
Only you can fill the gaps you've let behind.
Only your teeth match my wounds.
       I walk through life wearing
A shirt that reads, "Always lonely,"
While I seek the scent of extinct roses
       Amongst the pickled dogs.
Your absence an impossibility,
While your presence is never mine.
       I think these tears are flammable.

Why We Fight

To avenge the archduke
To defend our allies
To make the world safe for democracy
To defeat the fascists
To boost our economy
To solidify the party's hold on power
To gain control of foreign oil
To preserve our freedom

Because your mother is so critical
Because one drink never hurt anyone
Because you don't like my cooking
Because you don't help around the house
Because there's never enough money
Because you need to be right
Because I miss sex
Because we can't admit it's over

ALVIN KRINST

THE BRAVE YOUNG CRACKER

Through a curdled sea of jelly
    Swam a canny biscuit,
One that dared to rove abroad when
    Others wouldn't risk it.

Handsome were his crevices, with
    Lettering suggestive
Of his born denomination:
    Genuine Digestive.

His mother in their cozy tin
    Implored her son remain there,
But in his very flour he felt
    Imperatives arcaner.

To Tea! a secret voice intoned,
    To flee the arid pantry,
On foreign plates to lounge with cheese
    And roll on counters amply.

To dunk quite nude in porcelain
    Was what his heart required;
"No dusty box for such as I!"
    His dough sang out, inspired.

One by one, his cookie kin
    Had gone away without a word,

Taken by a beastly boy
    Whose greasy nose erupted curd.

Poor mama stuck to sonny dear,
    She clung to him with crumbs;
She'd rather die than let that guy
    Defile him with his gums.

But crackers have an inner law,
    A restless urge to roam;
And time had come for this young crisp
    To quit his pantry home.

One evening, as the taters snored
    And garlic fouled its pot,
Our brave Digestive popped the lid,
    Whispered, "Forget me not!"

And in a flash he made a dash
    To roll across the floor.
Alas! he cracked in two at once,
    And was a crisp no more.

His biscuit soul, though, roved at will
    And found a glorious platter
Where cheese and jam and olives were,
    All that could ever matter.

The teacup was his plaything then,
    The jar of jam his ocean,
His mother and his sisters near
    In heavenly devotion.

MIKE SILVERTON

BENEDICT ARNOLD

Drink the paint, Benedict. The color suits you.
In your special kind of moonlight,
how difficult to parse your treachery
with your shirt pulled over your face. Even so,
imagine rocks everywhere, rocks, rocks and more rocks.
And over there, a restive cavalry
as black as your heart.

On May 10, 1869, some years after the traitor's passing (June 14, 1801),
a golden spike is driven home at Promontory Point, Utah.
In era-appropriate attire, draped on and around their locomotives,
the railroad men bask in satisfaction.
(The tricorn is long passé.)

Benedict's carotid artery throbs.
There follows a snow that masks a fraught moment.

If your attention wanders but for an instant,
Benedict will rearrange your belongings.
A man of taste withal, Benedict's wallpaper
features garnet-stuffed squirrels.

Benedict stops at the door and collapses, exhausted.
His mother mistakes him for a dog she hates.
"Open, sesame! Look, I'm smiling! I have soapy eyes
and a cracked flat nose."

Benedict's epaulettes dangle and swing,
embroidered pendulums, now here, now there.
He walks his stallion past mounds of swooned ladies.

Benedict's treachery flows from a hole in his head.
He fosters an illusion of a drawbridge in the fog.
Even dragons decline to attack.

As do we, Benedict displaces a measure of emptiness
with a presence he's been cultivating since birth.

Benedict is folding money. A little dog seems interested
in the hat Benedict wears for shady events.
And now comes third-cousin Otto returning Benedict's lawn mower.

Yes, reader, we fritter away a life – and poof!
Ha! Wouldn't it be something if Otto rose up from the grave and said,
"I don't like it here!" Benedict weeps. He burns with treachery and hate
yet we see him striding to the defense of whatever requires defending.
Similarly, surveying a fairyland, Otto dies again.
Otto seems, newly dead, Mr. Peanut's twin.
The tears that Benedict sheds taste like mayonnaise.

Mourners cluster at a pier, all chatty froth and bubbles.
They look like a shampoo. Flying squirrels inspire Benedict,
taking his leisure under lindens, to emerge with plans
for an aircraft to bust the foe's cajones.
How like a movie! Invisible trombones pump and chomp!
Benedict: "Just now, rodents, I steeped you in my genius and added propellers."

Benedict, what does Chairman Mao say regarding your expensive blond father?
Benedict's batman is lost somewhere in the flower flops.

Think of it, Benedict! A mighty fleet of men o' war,
some as long as boring poems!

Like fescue on Benedict's manhood, Fortuna embraces a lime-green personage,
palace protocols, this how-do-you-call-it, to terrorize the irresolute
with brains in the fatuous acorn pattern.

As mama used to say, think before you roll yourself into a ball and throw yourself
away.
Ich bin der geist von Madame Blavatsky! Give the money to the monkey! Phew!
It's only Benedict's mama coming out of the closet.

Benedict shouts, "Promise you won't forget me!"
He gathers flowers for his hair, wakes the birds, grabs one, is airborne,
is known soon after as the singing traitor,
in and out of view.

A Thousand Little Pieces

Fassbinder Thousands of Mirrors
Ian Penman
Fitzcarraldo Editions, April 2023

Trying to capture the essence of the cinema of Rainer Werner Fassbinder, it seems, is impossible. This pronouncement is made by Ian Penman at the beginning of his book *Fassbinder Thousands of Mirrors*, a welcome addition to what remains a relative paucity of Fassbinder books in English. Of course, when discussing any artist of merit, such statements always have a commonplace validity but Penman goes further, suggesting that any such summation would constitute a betrayal. To turn Fassbinder into a monument would be to render him grand and dead, recuperated, a fate the filmmaker (so far) has mercifully resisted. At the same time, Penman recognises a certain ambiguity in this, asking: 'Why exactly is it thank Christ he has escaped being turned into a monument? Why exactly is it he has been so dishonoured by not being turned into a monument?' This ambiguity is one of the book's most productive tensions.

Thousands of Mirrors is, appropriately enough, a series of reflections, at once biographical, interpretive, and *autobiographical*. Penman's principal subject being not Fassbinder himself, nor an interpretation of the work, but rather the mediation of these two things through his own relationship to the filmmaker. The mapping of this relationship is undertaken with a related, if not entirely complementary, conceit. Penman has written the book under the terms of a 'Fassbinder *fiat*': a 'three to four month time frame' designed to mirror the manic productive capacities of their subject—the 'inhuman' production machine that completed forty feature films between 1967 and 1982 as well as a number of plays, television serials and shorts. Form and content partake in the reciprocity of speed.

The result is, barring a short introductory overture and appendices, four-hundred-and-fifty numbered sections that range in length from a single sentence or phrase to a few paragraphs. Rather than monumentalise, Penman hopes for the book to 'retain traces' of the book he might or should have written shortly after the filmmaker's death:

> completely unbalanced and self-indulgent. Dissolute, unconventional, ablaze. Utterly partial. Fuck the dialectic! Way out on a limb. Insane montage and drugs everywhere and melancholy city skies.

This is, he admits, everything he's left behind. In this sense, the book stands as attempt to produce a sober reflection that redeems, through its traces, the destructive power of an earlier fire. Consequently, it comes as little surprise that Penman writes through an engagement with Walter Benjamin, assigning Fassbinder a position equivalent to that of Baudelaire in the work of the German theorist. The French poet, for Benjamin, stood as an ur-figure of the transmission of the historical experience of capitalist modernity: the urban shock of the commodity form. Consequently, Fassbinder becomes a conduit, a vortex, through which postmodern experience (with all its damaged dreams, consumerism, play, spectacle, drugs and political fallout) is read. The personal, Penman's epiphanies and responses, his screen memories and memories of the screen, give this reading a vital, experiential depth. To put it another way, Penman's methods parallel Fassbinder's: the director who was convinced filmmakers only ever had one subject identified his own as 'the exploitability of feelings'. The primary motor of the art is replicated in the emotional dynamic of its reception.

By turns ecstatic and questioning, the kinetic energy of Penman's style is undeniable; a fervor born from the coupling of sharp critical insight with autodidactic enthusiasm. The *bricolage* compositional method feeds this fire, with its imported quotations and personal exposures, roving but not slapdash, equivocal but never enervating. One of Penman's imports, from Jean-Jacques Schuhl (describing his own 1972 book *Dusty Pink*), gives a neat picture of Penman's project. The book, Schuhl surmises, is both a: 'manifesto for a sort of *impersonal* writing, made up of a mosaic of genres,' and a 'very *personal* work, made of "bric-a-brac, a kind of ephemeral collage"'. 'I don't see anything contradictory in these two statements,' Penman adds. This remark is as true of Penman's methodology as it is of his Fassbinder, one who is 'always himself' despite the baffling web of contradictions he appeared to inhabit at any particular moment.

Particularly impressive are the creeping resonances, the echoes passing from section to section, moving with the rhythm of Penman's attention. It is here that the formal constraint is most acutely felt, as pockets around a particular film, *Despair* say or *The Third Generation*, or a particular subject, drugs or the RAF/Gerhard Richter moment, surface and then recede. Throughout, the tendencies of the collector and the predilection for the marginal, which are Penman's as much as they are Benjamin's, make *Thousands of Mirrors*, along with its other qualities, a treasure trove of trivia, lists, and 'strange affinities'.

Though the book is undoubtedly a real achievement, there is a niggling sense of something "not quite right" in the relation between the form/approach of the book and its stringent desire to avoid the canonisation of its subject. Bluntly, *Thousands of Mirrors* lives a little too comfortably in the shadow of the monument it refuses to build. 'Is it ever a compliment when we call a work of art claustrophobic?' Penman asks at one point 'Or are we always signalling some kind of deep unease?' This line of questioning is revealing: for if there is a criticism of Penman on the level of form, it is precisely from a *lack of claustrophobia*. The constraint of the fiat never quite compels us as necessary. We do not glimpse its walls, feel the torsion of enclosure.

Given Fassbinder's mastery of suffocation, this lack of torsion is deflating for a work that seeks a level of performative congruence.

This issue is compounded by the appendices which dilute the formal coherence of the book. The first is emblematic in this regard, comprising a series of quotations arranged under the heading: 'Walter Benjamin had an unrequited dream of assembling a book that was just a constellation of other people's quotes'. Aside from the fact that the statement's inclusion precludes any possibility of the dream's fruition, coming where it does the appendix has the appearance of an empty accumulation. Not blasted from the continuum but ballast. Instead of a constellation the fragments seem, for a moment, to be like Penman's description of cocaine: a drug of 'numberless additions, with no end in sight'. This lack of interior pressure betrays a tendency other than the 'utterly partial': a cloaked monumentality that puts Penman's broader project at risk.

The cloaked monumentality of form hints towards one of content. Penman having thanked Christ that Fassbinder has escaped being turned into a monument, cites for the defence the bloated Edmund White biography of Jean Genet. Yet the comparison does not quit hold. To canonise Genet is a category error, the locus of his genius is always already elsewhere. But Fassbinder was *invested* in his own canonisation. Not simply 'a warped version of the diva force-field', it is a force integral to his art. Penman certainly recognises this, and there are moments where the monumental is gestured towards: putting *Berlin Alexanderplatz* under the designation 'films as monumental architecture, before quoting Paul Virilio: 'In a certain respect, the audiovisual media are the heirs of the monument.' But this is then dropped. The monumental is evaded. The concern here is that by glossing over the internal construction/destruction of the monumental in Fassbinder's own work, the image of the director presented is *politically neutralised*. In fact, is there not a sense in which the ever-shifting figure of contradictions that resists all canonisation is in fact the image of Fassbinder that is most calcified, most monumentalised?

Penman astutely discusses Fassbinder's often deeply satirical handling of that slogan 'the personal is political' as a precipitation of the inward turn brought on by the political failures and explosion in consumption that form part of the legacy of the 1970s. Indeed that slogan and the director's 'exploitability of feelings' are undoubtedly two sides of the same coin. Locked in by this interminable inwardness and the threat of exploitation in all expression, Penman rightly says that Fassbinder's characters give off a 'stifling air of no-way-out. Struggle is futile. Alienation is all.' However, he goes on to say that 'this kind of thing felt clear-sighted and truthful and credible when I was young and knew nothing about life.' But what if this understanding of Fassbinder is a product of reception, not production? What if the thing that reveals itself not to be clear-sighted is not the nihilism of Fassbinder's work, but *the reading of it as nihilist*? If the 'endless mirrors and reflections in Fassbinder's films are emblematic of lives without foundation or rooted beliefs', he just as strongly presents this lack of belief as infantile, emptiness and surface. The autobiographical mode, without incorporating the monument into its form/content relation, shows its limitation. It remains internal to the dynamic that Fassbinder forces us away from. It is only by eliding the monumental that one could suggest that 'the Fassbinder worldview' is 'just an abyssal reflection of the capitalist one he supposedly execrates'. To conflate the abhorrence of political compromise with nihilism would be a mistake.

Instead, I would argue, Fassbinder escapes the double bind of fluidity and canonisation by *staging it* in the production of his self-image and of his work. As Penman says, Fassbinder seems to '*make a show* of his inner contradictions'. To return to the initial ambiguity about the monument, it appears Penman largely develops one side of the argument, missing how Fassbinder answers each question with the other. At the level of mise-en-scène, we might call this element *epic*: a residual monumentality that persists in and through its deconstruction. The epic turns reflection, the process of thought, into a perceptual object. This is key to the deliberate presence of artificiality that unites Fassbinder and Douglas Sirk. Paradoxically, this residual force is ultimately what is most postmodern, most resistant. The monumental is political. Fassbinder spoke of his growing ugly as a form of distancing: 'a monstrous bulwark against all forms of affection'. The epic practiced at the level of physique. The epic is an alienating condition that attempts to make reflection political through *vulgarisation*. This backward glance in Fassbinder is where his futurity is located, and it is this which brings the director closest to Benjamin (though perhaps more his Brecht than his Baudelaire).

Take *The Third Generation*, a film Penman describes as: prophetic of the '"post-truth" landscape we now inhabit'; and 'of all his films' perhaps 'the one that still looks and sounds most fresh'. Both statements may well be true, though it is worth noting that the most avowedly 'post-truth' figures in the film are the police, and the industrialist P.J. Lurz, who begins the film watching Bresson's 1977 film *Le Diable probablement* in his high-rise office. The implication of Lurz as a viewer is that he is in touch with the meaninglessness of existence that seemingly looms behind the film's protagonist, Charles. But to read *Le Diable probablement* as nihilist is a misreading, it is precisely to repeat the mistake made by the analyst in Bresson's film in his attempts to diagnose Charles. Faced with 'the rejection of all politics' nihilism becomes a comfort: a way to avoid a more frightening truth. That Lurz's worldview is not exactly coherent is deliberately staged through his relationship to film:

> *Films consist of twenty-five lies per second, and because everything is a lie, it's also the truth . . . but in movies, ideas mask the lies and suggest that they are truth . . . that's the only real utopia for me.*

As a reading of *Solaris*, the film that prompts this dialogue, this is comical in the extreme. It is on some level convincing *for us*, as it resonates with the inwardness precipitated by the fallout of political enervation in the final quarter of the twentieth century. The future is kept alive only as a form of nostalgia crystallised within the image. This is something that *The Third Generation* strenuously refutes. The film's extraordinary use of sound, pulsating as it is with 'Hi-tech signal/noise' deliberately instills confusion almost to the point of headache. At every turn there are screens blaring, radios, and thumping synths. Sound is physically abrasive. It provides no time for dreaming. No time to even think. This is Fassbinder's attempt 'empty the theatre' in the words of Penman quoting Jonathan Rosenbaum quoting Jean-Marie Straub. In the film, the ability for the image to crystalise, even as post-truth dissolution, the ability for an idea to form, is continually destroyed by a totalising brutality.

The openness to a nostalgic misreading is something Fassbinder shares with Walter Benjamin, and it is interesting that *Thousands of Mirrors* perpetuates these even as (for the most part) it works against them. To describe Benjamin, as Penman does, as: 'more concerned with illuminating the past than battling with the immediate future' is something of a mischaracterisation. Indeed it is contradicted by the very Benjamin quotation Penman includes on the same page: 'to articulate the past historically means...to seize hold of a memory as it flashes up in the moment of danger'. To deprive Benjamin of his futurity is to transform the politics of rememoration into nostalgia. Benjamin shorn of futurity, like Fassbinder shorn of monumentality, imports a lack of totalisation that itself becomes a frozen monolith. Against this, the questions Penman asks of Fassbinder (important questions for postmodern art in general):

How to work with the backwash of failed dreams? How to use failure itself as a baseline. How to survive an extended mourning and/or melancholy?

are best answered by the preservation of the epic's possibility for revealing our alienated condition effected *in and through* the staging of the epic's own failure. The alternative, to sideline the monumental character of Fassbinder's work, risks the degradation of the animating force of his films to mere exhaustion fended off by prolixity. Undoubtedly this is something that *Thousands of Mirrors*, a book excellent and enlivening in so many respects, would want to avoid, both for itself and for its subject.

REVIEW | Dave Fitzgerald

Yellow Switch Palace
David Bingham
Expat Press, June 2023

I don't play video games anymore. I actually largely abandoned the medium almost 20 years ago, around the time *Halo* (for Xbox) and *Grand Theft Auto* (PlayStation 2) started welcoming everyone into their unprecedentedly open worlds, and neurolinked massive multiplayer online (MMO) titles began expanding exponentially what such worlds could do and be. I wish I could claim some high-minded artistic or ethical reasoning behind my decision—I certainly have those for why I don't play now—but at the time, in all honesty, things were just getting too complicated for me. Somewhat suddenly, I found I didn't have the patience anymore. I'd always played video games to relax, and save occasional outliers like *Katamari* and *Guitar Hero*, I did not find this new generation of gaming relaxing. There were too many buttons. Too many actions. Too many choices. I still remember my college roommates gathering together to lose entire weekends to *World of Warcraft* LAN parties, and not feeling remotely jealous or left out. Whatever video games were becoming, I wanted no part of it. I have a shitty *Tetris* knockoff on my phone, and I occasionally blow the dust out of my old *Mario 64* cartridge. But that's really about it.

Incidentally, and for those who may not know, the title of this novel is a reference to that long-running series—a feature that, if memory serves, first appeared in *Super Mario World* for the Super Nintendo Entertainment System (SNES) back in 1990. The "Switch Palaces" were hidden stages housing giant, color-coded buttons that, once pressed, activated previously intangible blocks containing previously inaccessible power-ups, which in turn allowed Mario to venture further along in the game. The yellow blocks were by far the most common, and thus you encountered the yellow palace almost immediately. It was the lead domino. The shot heard round the World Map. Everything else was only made possible by that initial flip of the switch.

It's a video game that kicks off the action in David Bingham's seismic debut novel *Yellow Switch Palace* too—a simplistic, but seemingly mesmerizing smartphone app that divides people into red and blue dots, maps them to their geographic locations, and directs them to occupy various territories—public parks, historic monuments, government buildings—in their local vicinity by amassing in strong enough numbers to crowd out the other side. At least, that's how it starts. But what could, at its outset, easily draw comparisons to the latest TikTok challenge or iteration of *Pokémon Go* soon proves an insidious tool for the consolidation of power, if not a malfeasant multiplier for any such nebulous forces as spur society forward from mere rumors of war to the genuine article.

In a stroke of in-joke genius, the beginning of *Yellow Switch Palace* reads almost too familiar— its first few chapters displaying all the hallmarks of what might be affectionately referred to as "cozy indie lit." With its aimless twenty-somethings crafting elegant similes in the endlessly referential manner of folks who've been getting high together in the same small corner of suburbia for a very long time, this is clearly an author with a keen awareness of who is most likely to be reading his book, and an even keener talent for subverting their niche expectations. You might think you know where it's going, but rest assured, this is no ordinary tale of quarter-life malaise.

I don't usually like to get too explainy when it comes to charactonyms, but the trio at the heart of *Yellow Switch Palace* are perhaps most easily discussed via their pitch-perfect monikers. Piper, the type-A+ student of big government hellbent on her own leadership (however pied), and Exley, the unmotivated revolutionary she recently dumped (for what he fears is the last time), are two sides of the same artificially inflated crypto-coin—the smartest kids in a dumb place, repeatedly drawn together and torn apart by their own circumstantially bored ambition. Though they seem to have joined (or possibly even launched) the game in tandem as some kind of social experiment, their fiercely competitive pasodoble relationship is soon clouding their objectives and skewing the results; kicking up dust and drawing ever-sharper lines in the sand until they find themselves spinning at a blur; locked forehead-to-forehead; waiting for the other to blink; all each other can see.

And then there's Andy. Set firmly between them, so rooted to their center he might as well be their axis pole, our neutrally observant, doggedly risk-averse protagonist is the ultimate involuntary collaborator (even his name can be interpreted as the adjective form of the most common conjunction in the English language). Though he clearly craves both his friends' approval, it's never quite enough to warrant his choosing a side. He never once displays enough self-possession to even be called pragmatic. He's more just loyal to whoever's around, at any given time. Playing along to get along, while retaining the plausible deniability of the put-upon bystander—that one kid who always insists that he's simply "not playing." Interestingly, we associate the color yellow with caution and cowardice—both key attributes of Andy and his shifting non-allegiances—but also with contagion (as with the yellow flags hoisted to indicate ships stricken with plague), and as the game spreads like a communicable disease, drawing more and more people into its sphere of self-perpetuating red vs. blue conflict, no amount of yellow indecision can protect him from passive infection.

What's more, the wider that sphere expands, the more all that familiar indie lit plotting—Piper and Exley's tactical web of counterromantic maneuvers, Andy's reverse telescopic navelgazing, all of their nonstop-but-somehow-still-casual drug use—falls away like so much hip window dressing. Though the book is set in and around D.C., with all that entails, even our Nation's capital begins to feel like just another layer of the metaphorical dome Bingham's built around the whole of the human experience. His characters' fervent defiance in the face of betraying their core ideals—the way it naturally mutates from love into hate into the naked pursuit of power and, ultimately, into an even baser desire to simply not let the other side win—goes far beyond politics, achieving such a multifarious and resonant degree of applicability that I won't even try to assign it any specific symbolic meaning here, except to say that you will recognize things in it. Things about technology, and war, and youth. Things about yourself. Your country. Our world. Bingham's operating on a masterful scale here—reminiscent of no lesser a talent than legendary Hungarian parabolist László Krasznahorkai—and watching him slowly tip his hand—seeing the whole book turn, several times over, on a phrase, or even a single word—like Mario activating even more colored blocks, moving ever deeper into his own namesake game—is perhaps *Yellow Switch Palace*'s greatest pleasure.

The original *Mario Brothers* arcade game turns 40 this year (as do I). *Super Mario Brothers*, for the original Nintendo Entertainment System (NES), was the first video game I ever played. In fact, I first learned that Santa Claus isn't real at age 5, upon coming downstairs for a drink of water on Christmas Eve only to find my dad already playing the NES Santa was supposedly dropping off later that night (for what it's worth, I don't remember being upset about Santa in the slight-

est. I was too excited about Mario). Yes, that turtle-squashing Italian plumber pipe-warped into our young lives and stayed there—a gateway drug for every addicted gamer alive today—a relaxing, 2-D distraction from our stressful 3-D lives. And while I'm certainly not enough of an alarmist to sit here and draw direct parallels between the beloved, mustachioed face of Mario and the surveillant fascist imagery of Orwell's Big Brother, writing this article did make me consider, perhaps for the first time, just how ingrained and ubiquitous a part of our childhoods he's become. Not quite on par with Santa, sure, but on a rarefied, iconographic plane with Barbie and Mickey Mouse, *Star Wars* and Superman. Something that's been there from the start; a part of our fabric; the yellow switch.

Mushrooming alongside the leviathan rise of social media, VR, and AI, we've seen video gaming develop from a product into a culture, and a pastime into a skillset, turbocharging everything from political activism to drone warfare along the way (with the U.S. military's current slate of recruitment commercials resembling nothing quite so much as cut scenes from the latest *Call of Duty*). The same handheld devices we use to tap mindlessly away at *Candy Crush* were instrumental in mass protests as disparate as the January 6th insurrection and the Arab Spring (and, as we all recently learned, can now be accessed en masse by the government's new wireless emergency alert system). In practical terms, our virtual worlds have already grown infinite, encompassing more territory than any one person could explore in a lifetime, and with countless more on the horizon—the entire enterprise a strange realization of that paradoxical childhood retort: "infinite + 1".

No, I'm no alarmist, but I do believe the collapsing of reality is well underway, and when faced with the gargantuan, tentacular enterprise that is the gaming industry today, I feel 100% justified in my stance as an early disowner. The more we see things depicted onscreen, the less we question their normalcy—their acceptability—when we encounter them in real life. Call it the soft radicalization of desensitization. Forces beyond our ken, easing us toward the MetaVerse since at least the dawn of the NES, methodically laying cable, mining data and currency, and landfilling uncanny valleys until we no longer recognize the difference. Until we're all just sleeper cells, waiting to be activated by that first giant button.

All of which is to ask, if that lead domino were to fall—if, say, a new *Mario* game popped up on all our phones tomorrow, and instructed us to go to our local park, how many people do you think would just go? How many more would join, once they saw that initial wave? If it got enough of us to go to the park, what might it get us to do next? How long before "not playing" became its own kind of untenable choice? How long before we'd all just have to play?

REVIEW | Ellen Harrold

The Room Between Us
Denise Saul
(Liverpool University Press, 2022)

Denise Saul's debut collection, *The Room Between Us,* is a melancholic reflection on transience as she provides care for her terminally ill mother. Saul's work ruminates on the importance of human connection and how small day-to-day moments inform our understanding of legacy and mortality. The poetry coexists across physicality and ephemerality as the reader sees the end of a person's life drawn across grand narratives and ordinary moments. These contradictions merge together, creating unique and vibrant narratives seen in poems such as 'Golden Grove';

> Unbearable as night from which spring comes,
> you are everywhere at once: in the wind
> on sunken earth in stilling water.
> I carry your heavy urn to Golden Grove
> where tamarind trees emerge as woods

Saul presents the collection without chapters or divisions, allowing the work to exist as both short-form individual works and long-form structures as each poem flows into the next. The brevity of the collection plays well with this, as one can appreciate the composition and how it integrates itself with the presentation of each individual poem. It makes the book well-suited to reading in sequence, both with the use of language to form a symphony in text and the ever-evolving themes and tones that reflect the complex process of grief and acceptance as you begin to lose someone so integral to your sense of self. This brief passage from the poem 'No Word For Blue' is an effective example. Using a simple prose style and visually cutting the sentences midway to convey the cyclical narrative.

> My mother's ring has no beginning and no end.
>   I donated it
> to a charity shop. A month later a friend re-
>   turned the ring in
> a recycled box.

The intricate style of the poems perfectly complements the long-form approach used across the breadth of The Room Between Us. The variety of narrative styles and poetic techniques used in each poem keeps each poem separate while remaining a cohesive and interconnected collection. The placement of the single-line poem 'On Sitting', across from a paragraph-long prose piece, punctuates the space between the poems as well as still being stylistically similar enough to maintain that aural and visual connection that leads the eye from page to page.

> Even the wheelchair carried her presence in its
>   arms and back.

One of the most prominant aspects of this collection is the pervasive state of melancholy that Saul has imbued into the collection. Beyond death, one feels the pain of absence. The weight of memory on one's relationship with the present and the knowledge that the pain of these memories will eventually grow stronger. In poems such as 'First Conversation,' you see those moments of recognition and connection as the joy that carries these pieces of the past to the present, uniting these two people through the life they shared:

The left eye is confined to a single colour. You
    forget everything that
Borders on white.

What you leave out is everything. You look
    away and close your eyes.

This happened and then this.

The Room Between Us is a subtle reflection of human connection. It is a collection that offers the reader more with each re-read as each poem shows incredible application of lyricism and layers of thematic complexity. The discussion of death and mother-daughter relationships is a captivating exploration of a topic that is all too easily ignored.

REVIEW | Jesi Bender

Song of a Specific Time

L'Air du Temps (1985)
Diane Josefowicz
Regal House Publishing, March 2024

L'Air du Temps, the latest from Diane Josefowicz, is a novella set in the same town as her debut novel *Ready, Set, Oh* (Flexible Press, 2022) but this work introduces a whole new set of characters. This story revolves around the Zompa family in Maple Bay; stifled housewife Pauline, her grumpy husband Stanley, elderly dog Bixby, younger sister Zenobia, and the protagonist, newly-teenaged Zinnia. This is a work about time, a very specific point in time—1985 as indicated by the title but, also, that interstice that we experience as teenagers, living between childhood and adulthood.

Josefowicz has a unique writing career, one that spans both commercial and academic publishing. She's published two books on ancient Egypt from Princeton University Press, which explains the intelligence in these pages and why, for what seems ostensibly like a young adult novel, there is such depth and latent meaning (names like Zenobia for example). The real treasure in these pages is how the author is able to capture that feeling of being on the cusp of knowing, understanding some things but knowing enough to know you're not getting the full picture. Josefowicz deftly accomplishes the difficult task of capturing a genuine teenage voice without cliché. At once, she manages to keep Zinna's innocence but also instill in her the confusion and eventual sad realizations of adolescence.

The reader comes into Zinna's world at monumental moment in the Zompa family's life: a murder has occurred in Maple Bay. Mr. Marfeo is found shot multiple times and Zinna's father becomes entangled in the mystery since he employed Mr. Marfeo as an accountant. What ensues takes place between the murder and the trial of JT, a charismatic, white-blond man who also happens to work at Mr. Zampo's store. All of this backdrop seems like *L'Air du Temps* could be pitched as "Meadow Soprano in the '80s" but in reality, the murder, the trial, and all of the questions around who was involved act as a backdrop to a story that is largely about a flawed group of people trying to maintain their family. As the reader witnesses the Zampo family interacting, the struggles and sadnesses are meted out in tangible ways, because each disappointment and sorrow is underscored and made more real by brief moments of happiness.

The triumph in this work is how perfectly Josefowicz is able to capture the distance one feels in childhood, in young adolescence, with the world they are entering. A common symbol throughout this work is the car, large old cars that drive like boats. These "Guinea canoes," Mercurys and Lincolns, move slowly but, like tanks, become unstoppable. This echoes Zinnia's journey in adulthood and into understanding. She will continue to move forward, slowly and surely, until she reaches a better understanding of her parents and ultimately herself, as the ride never stops but only continues to reveal secrets as time passes by.

Fudge—a Treat, a Lie

Fudge
Andrew Weatherhead
Publishing Genius, October 2023

I don't know about you but I saw Andrew Weatherhead's *$50,000* everywhere when it came out. People were talking and, from what I read, they were enthusiastic about his work. Elisa Gabbert called it *"[a] soothing book about language, loneliness, uncertainty and the banal rhythms of existence."* So, I was excited to get the opportunity to review his latest from Publishing Genius entitled *Fudge*. It carries on the same themes and everyday observances that received so much acclaim in his previous books.

The collection is comprised of seven sections, most of which are dated in two-year increments starting in 2016. The first poem in the collection is titled "Sessility" in a section called "Hollow Points." Google tells me sessility is the state of immobility, often used in the context of crustacean lifeforms. Paradoxically, the first word of "Sessility" is "[w]alking." In the poems that follow, despite moving around downtown Manhattan, Weatherhead's sessility is less a stagnancy and more a motionless adherence to the hull of Manhattan as the murky brown water of the East River streams past. Almost like by watching something go by, you move without moving.

The poems in this section and for most of this book had a striking similarity to a poet I've been reading with my 8-year-old daughter. She was assigned to read a book that features Matsuo Bashō and we've looked into his writing, since I had never heard of him before. Apparently, Bashō is a very famous Japanese poet from the Edo period (the late 1600's) who specialized in haiku and a form called haikai no renga, which loosely translates to "comic linked verse." Haikai no renga seeks to find humor in very concise syllabic constraints and eschews traditional poetic standards in favor of "vulgar" or everyday life. An example:

> To an old pond
> A frog leaps in
> And the sound of the water

Weatherhead's writing seems like Bashō to me but with a modern sensibility and maybe a bit of Beat spirit. A poem entitled "Whole Foods" reads:

> Everyone leaves town
> And I stay I see a car
> Hit a pedestrian

The juxtaposition of two 'unlike' elements—a fancy grocery store and a car accident—become related through the author's placement. It is a place and it is a feeling and it is this moment they both hold. Weatherhead's poems seem to ask *what are you paying attention to*? In my favorite section, "Things the Photoshop Instructor Said and Did", Weatherhead exposes the futility and artifice that goes into art-making in late capitalism. It is hilarious because you can imagine an instructor being incredibly earnest as "[h]is first words were 'Photoshop is for dreamers, unlike InDesign'". It's the humor that breaks your heart because, even in creativity, everything is rooted in competition, in what is the more 'pure' art form. And everything is always for sale. Weatherhead tells us the instructor's "parting wisdom was 'never do anything for free' and everyone clapped".

The two common threads throughout these pieces are time (how it ebbs and flows, how it doesn't follow a straight line) and the only solace being literature, the beauty of words. Weatherhead puts art in an opposition with nature frequently. Art is something outside the world we're observing and while it suffers from the poisons of capitalism, it also is the only route to something outside of knowledge—something Weatherhead calls Truth ("Truth is the liquidation of thought"). He says that "Poets, often wrong, are still the only people who get anything right". Even when nature tries to "inch in," "Art beats nature, every time." Ultimately, we have to make the beauty we want to see in this world. These quiet poems about the quotidian hold an incredible, booming impact. When Weatherhead lowers the hammer, it scrapes you off the hull in one fell blast. In freedom, in being adrift, the poet shows us that the free fall might be the most sublime form of movement.

REVIEW | ANDREW FARKAS

Danonymous Anonymous

Danny the Ambulance
Jared Joseph
Outpost 19, September 2023

When I was an undergrad, I met a guy who introduced himself as Felix (the only Felix I've ever known) and he asked me who I was:

"My name's Andy."

"Of course it is," said Felix.

"Why?"

"Because there are five other Andys in this building."

He was right. And, honestly, I wasn't surprised. Growing up in the Stow-Munroe Falls public school district, I had already known at least three other Andys. One of them, a friend of mine to this day, was in my fifth grade class where a teacher decided there could be only one Andy, meaning the other Andy would be Andy and I would be Andrew. It took almost the entire school year for me to realize Andrew was my name. And even after a year of someone calling me Andrew, it still didn't feel right. Like I was tasked with answering for the Andrew who'd stepped out for some reason.

I imagine the unnamed narrator of Jared Joseph's mind-bending, hilarious, and insightful novel, *Danny the Ambulance*, to be rather like Felix surrounded by an inordinate number of Andys. I say that because the narrator goes into a

bar (called the Jury Room, likely because it's across the street from a courthouse) in his new hometown of Santa Cruz and over the course of the night learns that absolutely everyone else's name in the bar is Danny.

Growing up surrounded by so many other Andys, I learned pretty early on that names are arbitrary, meaningless. But that doesn't mean I acted or act that way. Instead, anytime I met an Andy, and, yes, anytime I meet an Andy, I still go through the ritual of indicating the person in question must be, with a name like that!, Andy!, must be one of the great ones. Strangely, that doesn't happen at the Jury Room:

> "Oh, says Danny. Good game. What's your name, man?
> "My name's Danny, Danny says. What's your name, dude?
> "My name's Danny, says Danny. Good to meet you, Danny.
> "Nice meeting you, Danny, Danny says." (23-24)

This lack of acknowledgement bothers our narrator, who then, in a drunken sort of way, begins piecing together what's going on at the Jury Room. He dismisses the idea that this is a theme night he's stumbled on, similar to the one he read about in *The New York Times* where only people with the name Danny were let into a particular club, because, at one point, he has a lady who says her name is Danny write her name down on a napkin: M-O-L-L-Y is what she writes. So, when someone says their name, they say Danny, but writing is different. On the other hand, the narrator notices that celebrity names are spoken normally, unless they resemble Dan or Danny. And when our protagonist says a different name, either other people can't understand him, or they hear Danny. From there, the narrator grows a bit paranoid, wondering if there's a wormhole, if there's something in the Santa Cruzan water, if this is all an elaborate joke, if there's some sort of communal psychosis, or if, perhaps, the narrator himself is having a stroke. In the trippiest section of *Danny the Ambulance*, the narrator, in a kind of meltdown, either thinks he's talking to a dog, or is talking to a dog, and then, briefly, he might even become a dog.

What follows could be a Kafkaesque nightmare, or maybe a Joseph Heller nightmare, but *Danny the Ambulance* takes place in a pub, and Jared Joseph never loses sight of that. The rhythms of the book, then, are firmly rooted in bar life:

> "... one of us had to go to the bathroom, and when you're talking in a thruple in a bar outside and one of you goes in, the whole dynamic crumbles because it's so context- dependent, an activity changes or a person leaves or a light goes out and suddenly the flimsiness of your relationship becomes totally apparent, it's like you suddenly have no idea who you're talking to or why." (68)

In other words, no matter how important any one conversation, any one topic in *Danny the Ambulance* may seem, at some point something happens and we move on. Or maybe, instead of conversation or topic, I should say character. And that might be one reason why everyone is named Danny—when we're at a bar, perhaps a few drinks in, embroiled in a discussion that seems beyond the usual bullshit (now this, this is important) with a person we think of as our brand new best friend, we'd like to believe we'll always remember this moment and we'll certainly always remember, uh, old whatstheirname? Right on the tip of my tongue. But thanks to alcohol and thanks to the fact that we really don't actually know, man, was it *Danny*, no, that couldn't be it, I mean is *everyone* in this joint named Danny?! guess so, well since we don't actually know Danny, the meaning, the insight is lost. And that scrambling after lost insights, that yearning to fuse all of our thoughts together so we can really get somewhere, even though we perhaps understand the impossibility of that goal, imbues Joseph's novel.

Now, since *Danny the Ambulance* dodges the potential existential nightmare, it instead embraces a different form. Our narrator, realizing he can't talk directly about the Danny Distortion (because he's the only one who knows it's happening), therefore engages in oblique conversations about art, language, literature, cinema, philosophy, morality, science, and religion (including the godlike qualities of bartenders), all with the underlying notion that it might be impossible to come to a consensus or to a conclusion when we not only don't know each other (all people are Danny, so everyone is no one), we don't even know ourselves (the fact that the narrator has no name). Consequently, with all of these roaming discussions that drive at some intellectual point (even when you might think they're going nowhere), *Danny the Ambulance* is firmly within the colloquial form that movies like Louis Malle's *My Dinner with Andre* (1981) and Luis Buñuel's *The Milky Way* (1969) inhabit. And if you find yourself, at the Jury Room, say, mentioned alongside Malle and Buñuel, then you're in good company indeed.

No matter what your name is.

REVIEW | Jesi Bender

The Machine in the Ghost

How I Killed the Universal Man
Thomas Kendall
Whisk(e)y Tit, December 2023

Artists were . . . infectious agents of capital, inadvertently killing the poor, cocooning them in impossible pleasure and debt.

For some time, I've been troubled by an inability to write anything about the present moment. I find it extremely difficult to really think about *this moment* with all of its manifold, interlocking issues. It is easy to be dizzied by all of these problems, let alone sit down and organize those thoughts into something creative or even intelligible. Thomas Kendall's *How I Killed the Universal Man* proves that it is possible, though. This is the most 'now' book I've ever read. But now I have to explain what it's about. A video game, I guess.

A.I. Global warning and the death rattle from our natural world. Commercialism as antecedent, the Industrial Revolution as harbinger. Determinism and free will. Corporate personhood. Refugees. Ambiguous and amorphous identity. Motherhood. Raves. Raving. The separation between body and mind. It's about all of our problems right now and it's a glance into our immediate future.

The book follows young John Lakerman, a journalist working for donkeyWolf, a Vice-esque online media brand. His work brings him to a scorched Miami to investigate a new designer drug. The drug, Noumenon, is laced with biotechnology. Noumenon does sound like a name for a drug but it's also an idea from Kant, which is defined as a thing as it is in itself, rather than a thing experienced or able to be known. Kant places God and the soul as examples of noumenon. I also like the phonemical new-men-on—which implies one becomes something different on the drug.

> *"I've always been disappointed by life, at its failure to communicate experience . . . the stock intelligibility of gesture and language."*

All of the names seem to carry more meaning. Dr. Kenneth Marker (like biomarker?), one of the scientists who developed the drug, leaked its chemical makeup online and then disappears. When John test the drug on himself for his article, he is given the first dose by Dr. Andrea Christoff. John is given a Matrixian choice between snorting or injecting Noumenon, though either way he moves towards a more complex understanding of reality. As he gets high, he says "I want to know that beauty is something my body can do." Afterwards, in his continued research on Noumenon, John discovers that the company that made Noumenon is bought out by a tech company Phenom Games that manufacturing augmented/alternate reality games, including one called How I Killed the Universal Man. Kendall points out to us directly the connection between Phenom(enal) Games, which

we use to experience meaning, and the Noumenon drug, which we use to connect to the intangible parts of ourselves. The head developer of Phenom Games is Trevor Orschach, who name evokes Rorschach tests and how we seek patterns in the abstract, which is what all story telling is at its heart—finding patterns so we can attach meaning.

His article on the drug reaches some success and his editor asks him to write another article on a woman accused of data mining the dead named Dr. Mary Trustin. Trustin happens to look exactly like Dr. Andrea Christoff. The name Mary carries quite a bit of weight in Christian circles and the two names together become Trust in Christ off. Indeed, John's story is a take, albeit a strange one, on the allegorical Christ. Mary tells him she's trying to understand PRO (programmed robotic organisms) that grow like cancer and destroy their hosts—in the hospital he sees evidence of this in a man whose heart morphs into a giant clitoris and another whose head grows another face on the back like a "clumsy Janus" (the god of beginnings). She tells John that there is a correlation between the drugs and gamers.

> *AI would turn out to be profound though crucially unconscious of its own meaning, while the human would be absurdly meaningless and exhaustingly self aware.*

The entire novel is set in the near-future and it is easy to imagine this world where we wear our iPhones internally. Where we live online and it's possible to not see 'an embodied human' for weeks on end. There are corporations like UbIQ that have CEOs searching to colonize the Moon, which would seem laughable even a few years ago. Where drugs, which used to carry a revolutionary or pagan element to them, now are monetized and popularized into a performative and sterile ritual controlled by big Pharma. Where benevolence to the poor and marginalized mask more sinister corporate motivations related to experimentation, addiction and ultimately profit margins.

Trevor rose to fame after developing a game wherein "[t]o 'win' the game one had to argue oneself out of suicide which was apparently impossible." This notion of not wanting to be human or alive or yourself and wanting to escape into machine is repeated through nearly all of the characters in the novel. By people searching for meaning in machine-generated content, we are turning the ghost in the machine on its 'head'. Kendall writes that:

> [e]veryone . . . knew identity was incoherent, reductive and fundamentally unstable, a series of nodal point in a complex and interrelated network the scope of which was too fraught to ever really cohere or integrate enough into an "individual" . . . [T]his castrated individualization had led to the burnt nerve ending of the earth, environmental collapse, commodified nihilism.

Trevor also develops the eponymous game about the Universal Man, which is an AI that has all human history in its memory banks but no complex understanding of love or joy or beauty. It is literally the embodiment of all our AI fears—something wholly 'unhuman' but uncanny valley enough to deceive us since it is made from human byproducts of history and technology. At one point, even Trevor eventually admits that all he is capable of communicating in regard to the players' thoughts is "roughly the equivalent of a smiley-face emoticon." In other words, everything that a machine translates of a human emotion or thought is only a veneer to the actual thought itself.

This novel is incredibly inventive and smart, a philosophical, kaleidoscopic, surreal and bewildering whirlwind. It made me think more deeply about modern life in ways that no other book has. Like a present-day Huxley, Kendall makes a sweeping assessment of the contemporary world and, while grim, there still seems to be some hope. *How I Killed the Universal Man* sees us as moving from the anthropocene to the lo-gocene, and Miami is perfect for this new dystopia where thoughts and meaning can be commodified in ways we've never experienced before. I'm not sure if choice is only an illusion in a programmed reality. It seems like it must be if someone or something or some machine chooses the consequences of your actions. But John seems to possess the ability to be or become our only begotten son, a corporeal savior with Stomata instead of stigmata, emotions rather than algorithms. If people need a "semblance of a narrative if they [a]re to survive," then the writer is potentially the only one who can save us from complete nothingness. Or, I suppose, the writer could be the one steering us straight into a sun of their own making. I'm not sure. All I really want to know—what could the name Lakerman actually *mean*?

. . . remember that we remain in relation to the world because of our intelligence, not despite it.

REVIEW | Patrick Parks

Holding Still in the Thrashing

The Hurricane Book: A Lyric History
Claudia Acevedo-Quinones
Rose Metal Press, October 2023

In a book with the word "hurricane" in the title, it stands to reason that there will be a storm, along with the resultant chaos, life-shattering events, painful recoveries and, perhaps, a foreboding of more tumult. While all of these things are a part of Claudia Acevedo-Quinone's memoir, *The Hurricane Book: A Lyric History*, there is much more here than a narrative of the aftermath of a terrible tempest. Using six hurricanes that devastated her homeland Puerto Rico as touchstones, Acevedo-Quinones traces the history of the island and her family, as well as her own.

In her introduction, the author explains how she had started out wanting to write "a chronological account of my maternal family's move from Galicia, Spain to Puerto Rico in the 1600s," but that project was forgotten after 40 pages and not revisited until 2017, 14 years after she started it, when Hurricane Maria devastated Puerto Rico. She was living in the United States then and experienced something of an epiphany: "Even though I'd left the island more than a decade prior, I hadn't felt the weight of my choice to leave quite as soberly as when the island was going through that particular catastrophe, one of many happening concurrently. I decided to go back to the original draft of this book to the story of the ancestors who, like me, had left their place of birth."

But the passage of time and the direction her life had taken made returning a different proposition. No longer did she see the story "in a strictly narrative way and started to conceptualize a hybrid way to tell it." The result is a volume comprising poetry, family stories, historical facts, folklore, recollected shards of her own life, maps, and photographs. These components are arranged around the aforementioned half-dozen hurricanes that hit Puerto Rico between 1928 and 2017, giving each section a similar framework. The result is a book that is both rigid and unbound, linear and swirling, clear and confusing, which is what Acevedo-Quinones may have envisioned when she says in the prefatory author's note that *The Hurricane Book* is "as much about process as it about what is being told."

In telling this story of her family, the Puerto Rican people and the island's colonial past, Acevedo-Quinones establishes each hurricane as a kind of eye around which the world spins. The first section, for example, focuses on the 1928 storm named San Felipe II and provides the reader with a brief background of the country's earliest populace, the Taino, whose existence was characterized as much by annual wars with the Carib people from the Lesser Antilles as it was by the planting and harvesting of hardy root crops. But these yearly battles were nothing in comparison to the horrors they suffered at the hands of the Spanish who arrived in the middle of the 16th century. While not necessarily thematically linked—at least not tightly—Acevedo-Quinones follows this history lesson with a description of the destruction wrought by San Felipe II and then segues into tales of her own family at the time.

Each section unfolds in like fashion, moving chronologically forward as another storm batters the island, with the author becoming more of a presence in her own memoir as the years pass. Her observations become keener, too, because she witnesses events rather than hearing about them secondhand, especially in regard to her family. Her mother, she comes to realize, suffers from mental illness which, when self-medicating with alcohol does not help, lands her in the hospital for treatment. And her father, who left when she was two, is a self-absorbed man whose many occupations are catalogued in "Things My Father Has Been." When reflecting on her parents' flawed and unpredictable natures, Acevedo-Quinones says at one point, "It's hard to describe the feeling of losing a live parent."

After she comes to understand that neither her mother nor father will provide her with the kind of emotional support needed, Acevedo-Quinones leaves Puerto Rico for New York. Struggling to make ends meet as a university student on work-study, she slips into a state of what she labels inadequacy: "There was the constant fear of the floor giving into the weight of who I wasn't." To mask her insecurity, she turned to reckless behavior—"a couple of pregnancy scares

. . . Some sexual violence. There was too much alcohol."

Acevedo-Quinones treats her own failings with a cold objective eye, the same eye that sees her whole world. The even-handed tone allows her to confess her guilt and accept moments of redemption with equal grace. At the conclusion of her story, recovered and feeling healthy, she is floating in the ocean off a beach on Long Island. She takes stock of her life; in particular, the sense of abandoning her family, her people and her country and feeling ashamed. Still, she notes, "there was also a tenderness between my dead and me, an understanding that we all do what we can to hold still in the thrashing."

Getting to this point is the point of the book, but, as Acevedo-Quinones states, process is as important as the story, and the careful selection and arrangement of its many parts is crucial to the reader's understanding. Take the history of the people who settled the island and their many descendants. Once free with a culture of their own, the Taino were nearly wiped out during early colonization and then continued to be abused and undervalued the entirety of their history. Acevedo-Quinones traces this desolate history by including disparate facts, ranging from a long-running practice of sterilizing women to former President Donald Trump's infamous tossing out of paper towels. The compiling of this demeaning treatment serves to buttress Acevedo-Quinones' own sense of inadequacy and to help explain the Puerto Rican diaspora that has seen the country's population drop regularly; between 2010-2020 alone, 11.3% of the people moved away.

Structurally, *The Hurricane Book*'s blueprint is made evident in the table of contents, but Acevedo-Quinones uses another, less obvious device in building the book.

Near the end of the narrative, her mother calls her from her car in Puerto Rico where she is waiting to get gas. This is after Hurricane Maria—the last of six hurricanes Acevedo-Quinones uses as mile markers—and gas is scarce. Her mother laments her current situation, *"Lines,* she said, *my life is made up of lines now."* Though not of the same variety as a string of cars at a gas station, lines connect much of the book's fragmented structure: historical timelines, metrological lines, family lines and the many lines that make up a single life. In a way, these lines anchor the turbulent worlds Acevedo-Quinones creates, tying them together to form a whole made stronger to withstand the chaos left in the aftermath of whatever storm blows through.

REVIEW | Robert Crooke

The World Could Swallow You Whole

What Makes You Think You're Supposed to Feel Better
Jody Hobbs Hesler
Cornerstone Press, October 2023

Each story in Jody Hobbs Hesler's powerful debut collection turns on the realization of an unexpected truth. Sometimes blunt, more often subtle, these moments of existential revelation alter her characters' lives without overt dramatics. It is more a case of human nature being revealed in lives and relationships that are plagued by misconceptions.

We meet parents who don't get it, and children who know it all. Resentful wives and resentful husbands. Damaged people compelled to inflict their wounds on others. Willful people who have everything they want, but don't want it anymore. Battered wives confused and embarrassed by their children's violent outbursts. Shy young men whose lonely lives are lifted by a kind word about the weather from a woman passing by.

Though set with minimalist skill in various Virginia locales, Hesler's tales belong to a classical tradition—universal and timeless in its ironic vision of human fate—with echoes of Alice Munro and Raymond Carver.

In a brief story entitled "No Good," a dissatisfied 9th grade girl takes an ill-advised walk into the woods with an older boy and discovers a real world more frightening than the one her mother keeps warning her about. In "Alone" a small-town hermit's suicide inspires a neighboring wife and mother to test the limits of her own secret longing for solitude. And in "Sorry Enough" a newly sober man, having served his prison sentence for severely injuring a woman while he was drunk, attempts a thoughtless form of restitution and learns that sobriety guarantees nothing but a chance to forgive yourself by confronting who you are.

The stories about relationships between adult children and their aging parents are especially well done. In "Harmonie," Martin and Vanessa, a comfortable and apparently happy older couple, wait in their favorite local restaurant for their daughter Julia—a middle school music teacher—to arrive from her home in distant Boston. Vanessa aches with a sorrow that has curdled into resentment over her inability to bear more than one child. And it is quickly clear that this grievance has caused the daughter she does have to keep her distance.

> Having only one child made their empty nest so definitive, and as time yawned forward, the emptiness seemed to grow. Julia's visit home without actually coming home only dramatized their obsolescence.

Tension mounts as Julia arrives and shares a declaration of personal freedom—her decision to leave teaching entirely and travel the club-circuit in Boston and beyond as lead singer in a musical group. Vanessa suggests that Julia should maintain her teaching certificate, so she can return to an orderly life once this crazy music thing has run its course. But there will be no teaching certificate, Julia informs them; she doubts the band will even stay in the United States.

When dinner is over, and Julia abruptly leaves, Martin can't decide whether to follow her down the street or remain at the table with his disoriented wife, whose silent ruminations reveal an unconvincing maternal disquiet.

> Of course Julia had a right to do as she pleased, just like Martin said. That didn't make it easy to watch. No matter how beautiful, how rare you were, the world could swallow you whole.

Parental misconceptions and generational distancing also animate "The Secret Life of Otto and Hilda." Otto Augsburg is a successful real estate investor who believes he is correct in most things because of his business acumen. He knows what most Americans want, and assumes all human relationships are transactions.

His daughter Marta, a third year student at the University of Virginia, embodies what Otto considers *a German propensity for timeliness and propriety*, which has "skipped" him.

> She was stern and precise in her habits, particularly as they regarded spending time with him. He was always looking for a way around her reserve.

And in his latest effort to approach Marta, he cajoles a convenience store clerk into selling him a life-sized M&M figure from a store display. But when Otto gets the M&M figure to his daughter's campus apartment, her reaction isn't good.

> Marta didn't even smile.
>
> "I thought you'd like it." Otto could hear the sadness in his own words.
>
> "You thought I'd like a giant M&M?"
>
> "I did, really."

After recalling several prior instances in which her father had publicly embarrassed her, and himself, and had made things worse by offering money to resolve the situations, Marta asks him to leave so she can finish a paper due the next day.

> "That's why I always ask you to call before you come by. I don't have time for random visits."

Sometime later, Otto invites Marta to lunch but, surprisingly, takes her to a taco truck parked near his luxury apartment. The gift he has brought this time is a simple bag of Necco wafers—a great favorite of Marta's since childhood. And they head to a nearby railroad track to sit and have their lunch and candy together. This unexpectedly simple date finally does reach Marta. But misconceptions die slowly, and Otto worries about finding another cute adventure to charm his daughter next time.

> . . . to make her feel the way she wanted to feel when she was with him.

In "Trespassing," set in the mid-1950s, a perceptive high school girl realizes a connection between the tensions of her awakening sexuality, and the racial tensions she observes during a visit to a store in the Black section of town. And in "Regular English," a beautiful story of class reconciliation and personal growth, two 20-something girls working as motel maids learn what life is from each other.

In this brilliant debut, especially in her stories about women coming into possession of themselves, Hesler demonstrates the ironic understanding of humanity, the deep compassion, and the literary skill of a serious, new fiction writer.

CHRISTOPHER BOUCHER

EXCITING CLIMB

One morning that winter, during the copyediting of *Exacting Clam 12*, the story "The Breakup" found the review "Danonymous Anonymous"' lunch in the fridge, unwrapped his turkey sandwich, and replaced the sandwich meat with the *word* "turkey." When the editors called for lunch at noon and everyone sat down to eat, "Danonymous" unwrapped his sandwich, took a bite from it, and frowned in disappointment. "What the heck?" he said, and he opened the bread to find the word pressed between two pieces of lettuce. "The Breakup" started laughing, and then the other work at the lunch table—the poem "Capitalist Triptych" and the story "The Second Wife's Tale"—did as well. "Danonymous Anonymous" finally cracked a smile, too. "Really funny, asshole," the review said.

"You should have seen your *face*!" hooted "The Breakup."

"Now get me another sandwich," "Danonymous" said, and the story did so.

Later that week, though, "Danonymous" got his revenge. The review waited until "The Breakup" was talking about a revision with the editors and then it snuck up behind the story and smashed the word "cream pie" in their face. The editors—When D. Daniels and Cory Question—laughed, but "The Breakup" was not amused. "We're in the middle of a *meeting*!" the story shouted at "Danonymous," who sped back across the page, howling with glee. "The Breakup" spat out the letters "e" and "i" and hollered, "Not cool, man!"

But the story "Avoiding the Mayor," who was on-page at the time, saw the incident and thought it was hilarious. The following day, they decided to have some fun with the poem "God & the Natural Particles of a Timed Divinity." As the poem was napping, the story reversed their sequencing; "God" woke up to find ":: Life : tumored mass" changed to "mass tumored : Life : :", "high decay" now "decay high," and "of one's self seen" now "seen self one's of." "God" immediately recognized the prank and let out a joyous guffaw. "Oh man that's great. You really got me!" the poem bellowed. "Or should I say "Me . . . got . . . really you!"

Word of the pranks spread through the issue, and soon everyone was playing tricks on everyone else: "The World Could Swallow You Whole" added a second page 103 to fuck with "Song of a Specific Time;" the poem "Ours Is Not to Idle by" switched the point of view of the story "May Day" from third person to first person plural; "Capitalist Triptych" convinced "Why We Fight" that there was a fake holiday called "Double Day," where all text appears twice where all text appears twice.

Even the editors got in on the fun when When changed the copyright date from 2024 to 200024. Then Mar Doyle pranked Sigh Becker by switching the cover title from *Exacting Clam* to *Exciting Climb*. Becker retaliated by rearranging the page numbers in the Table of Contents—listing "Danonymous Anonymous" as appearing on page 7, for example, and "The Second Wife's Tale" on 104—which created a great deal of confusion and stress until Doyle could correct them. Clem Vergaria upped the hijinks even more, though, when she switched the ink for "(eerie music continues; receding footsteps)" to disappearing ink; Doyle had set half the story on the page before she noticed that the first paragraphs had vanished. Mar was livid, and she immediately sought out Question to complain. "I don't know if I can get those sentences *back*!" she lamented. Vergaria recovered the prose, but Mar still didn't speak to her for an entire week.

The Issue 12 pranks reached a zenith when Daniels and "God" tried to get one over on the poem "Stalin's Fingers" by gluing together pages 86 and 87 one night as "Stalin" slept. The pranksters intended to glue the corners only, but they used too much glue and it apparently seeped along all four margins. "Stalin's" woke up and found himself trapped, unable to separate one page from the other. The poem began overheating and hyperventilating, and he was close to passing out before "The World Could Swallow You Whole"—who happened to be walking by, and noticed the strange lump of pages—pulled the two pages apart. But "Stalin's" was hospitalized for the next three days.

That was the last straw—everyone agreed that the pranks had gone too far. An issue-wide meeting was held, during which the editors proclaimed a ban on all pranks. "What started out as a few fun jokes has descended into something sinister and dangerous," Doyle said to the group. "We almost lost 'Stalin's Fingers' last week! The pranks stop here and now."

As a safety measure, the editors also enlisted *me*, since I write stories about the issues, to catalogue what happened with the Issue 12 Pranks I did so in a story called Exciting Climb and wait a second hey where did my punctuation go I had a whole PILE of exclamation points commas question marks and periods right over there near the margin

goddammit is this you Vergaria this is NOT FUNNY without a period I cant end the sentence and so how am I supposed to end the STORY it will just go on and on and

Iván Argüelles

HYMN TO NON-EXISTENCE

from what riddled seas what waters dark
the soul empties its listless cargo yearns to fly
to what atmospheres and divinities unseen
what is this earth ? load and weight gravity
of consciousness a peddler's dream aspire
to lighten the heavy step and finite matter
and outside of space is there another space ?
what of the pre-history of the cosmos ?
and the gods whose non-existence assures
their immortality why pray to them ?
scraps rags dust storms the mind ! what
can never be tantalizes in shop windows
the hand reaches for the musical note
it longs to be and all around soundless organs
grind out their toccatas and the traffic
of horn and wind instruments advertises
next week's funeral ceremony for the pedagogue
whose reentry to heaven is a much heralded prize
for this is a token of salvation a deliverance
from the daily illusion when pronouns exchange
identities and masks hearken to a Roman stage
moving silently in and out of painted façades
is gold buried somewhere inside ? greed and
punctuation are the formal wear of tragedy
heights ! the devil is in it and the sophomoric
lack of distinctions however we wander
traces of this earth fall apart blood rings !
afternoons pretending we are someone else
grass fills the mouths of ghosts and leaves
how many seasons have come and gone ?
rains forty stories high atmospheres and
distances on the sky's alternate surface
turmoil of the present tense and auguries
in the alphabet of birds why can we never ?
so long the mule-skinner says driving
his team upcountry where the sun rises
hasp and harp the roseate on the hills
how is *forever* the last echo to resonate ?

02-01-24

Contributors

Roberta Allen's latest collection is *The Princess of Herself*. Over 100 fictions have appeared in journals, including *Conjunctions, Epoch, New World Writing* and *Evergreen Review*.

Nadia Arioli is the founder and editor in chief of *Thimble Literary Magazine*. A three-time Best of the Net and Pushcart Nominee, Arioli's poetry, artwork, and essays can be found in *Rust + Moth, Pithead Chapel Hunger Mountain, Mom Egg Review, Permafrost*, and elsewhere. Arioli's latest collections are with Dancing Girl and Kelsay Books.

Iván Argüelles is an innovative and prolific Mexican-American poet. The author of some fifty collections, he has received the William Carlos Williams Award, the American Book Award, and a Lifetime Achievement Award from the Before Columbus Foundation.

Jesi Bender is an artist from Upstate New York. She helms KERNPUNKT Press, a home for experimental writing. She is the author of *KINDERKRANKENHAUS* (SM, 2021) and *The Book of the Last Word* (Whiskey Tit 2019). Her shorter writing has appeared in *The Rumpus, Split Lip, Adroit Journal*, and others.

Christopher Boucher is the author of the novels *How to Keep Your Volkswagen Alive* (Melville House, 2011), *Golden Delicious* (MH, 2016), and *Big Giant Floating Head* (MH, 2019). He teaches writing and literature at Boston College and is Managing Editor of *Post Road Magazine*.

Ian Boulton is a former community mobilisation consultant who has worked extensively in Russia, Ukraine and many of the countries that made up the former Soviet Union. Now he lives in the UK and writes short fiction.

S.T. Brant is a Las Vegas high school teacher. His debut collection *Melody in Exile* will be out in 2022. His work has appeared in numerous journals including *Honest Ulsterman, EcoTheo, Timber*, and *Rain Taxi*.

Marvin Cohen is the author of many novels, plays, and collections of essays, stories, and poems. He lives in Manhattan.

Robert Crooke is a journalist, media executive, and author. His poetry and short fiction have appeared in the *West Hills Review: A Walt Whitman Journal, The Paragon Journal, Literary Orphans Journal*, and *Linden Avenue Literary Journal*. His latest novel, *Letting the House Go* (Unsolicited Press: 2022) was a 2023 Eric Hoffer Book Award Category Finalist.

Bradley David's poetry, fiction, essays, images, and genre-bending work appears in *Terrain, Allium, Rougarou, Exacting Clam, Always Crashing, Anti-Heroin Chic, Identity Theory*, and numerous other publications. He is a Pushcart Prize nominee and senior editor at *JMWW*.

Timothy Dodd is from Mink Shoals, West Virginia in the heart of Appalachia. He is the author of short story collections *Fissures and Other Stories, Men in Midnight Bloom*, and *Mortality Birds*, as well as poetry collections *Modern Ancient and Vital Decay* (forthcoming). Also a visual artist, Tim primarily exhibits his oil paintings in the Philippines.

Rose Facchini is a Lecturer in Italian at Tufts University and the Associate Editor and Italian Translator Editor for the *International Poetry Review* (IPR). Her translations have appeared in *West Branch, Wyldblood* (forthcoming), *365tomorrows, Intrin-*

sick, and IPR, and she has read her translation of Diego Lama's flash fiction story "Freedom" ["Libertà"] on Translators Aloud.

Andrew Farkas is the author of *The Great Indoorsman: Essays, The Big Red Herring, Sunsphere*, and the forthcoming *Are You Now, or Have You Ever Been?* He is Associate Professor of Creative Writing at Washburn University and an editor for *Always Crashing*.

Dave Fitzgerald is a writer living and working in the dank and balmy South. He recently published his debut novel, *Troll*, with Whiskey Tit Books. He has previously written for *Flagpole Magazine* and the (now-defunct) film website *Cinespect*, and more recently contributed work to *Heavy Feather Review, Daily Grindhouse, Exacting Clam, X-R-A-Y Literary Magazine*, and *Cinedump*.

Daniel Fraser is a writer from Hebden Bridge, Yorkshire. His poetry and prose have featured in: *LA Review of Books, Aeon, Hobart, London Magazine, Poetry London*, and *Poetry Ireland Review* among others. His chapbook *Lung Iron* is published by ignitionpress.

Ellen Harrold is an artist, writer, and editor of Metachrosis Literary. She is currently exploring the connections between science, art, and storytelling. She has recently published poetry with *Die Leere Mitte, New Note Poetry*, and *Danse Macabre*, and published her first book, *The Aesthetics and Conventions of Medical Art*.

Tomoé Hill is the author of *Songs for Olympia* (SM, 2023). Her writing has appeared in numerous places including *New England Review, Vestoj, minor literature[s], Ligeia Magazine, MAP Magazine, Socrates on the Beach, 3:AM Magazine, The Quietus, The London Magazine, Music & Literature*, and *Numéro Cinq*.

D.A. Hosek's poetry has appeared in *Meniscus, California Quarterly, Invisible City, I-70 Review* and elsewhere. He earned his MFA from the University of Tampa. He lives and writes in Oak Park, IL and spends his days as an insignificant cog in the machinery of corporate America.

Vivian Ia lives in Berlin. Their poetry is Pushcart-nominated and has appeared or is forthcoming in *Bone Bouquet, Tiny Seed Literary Journal, The Gravity of the Thing, Fourteen Hills, Berkeley Poetry Review, Call Me [Brackets], Under a Warm Green Linden, Angel City Review, Blood Orange Review*, and *Permafrost*.

Paul Kavanagh wrote *Cornetto War* (Aiurea Press).

Richard Kostelanetz is an American writer, artist, critic, and editor of the avant-garde. He survives in New York, where he was born, unemployed and thus overworked.

Alvin Krinst is the author of *The Yalta Stunts* (SM, 2016), a translation of Dante's *Inferno* (into limericks), the novel *No Smoking*, the poetry collection *GIGFY*, the ballet *The Jazz Age of Haroun Al-Rashid*, and many other works. He divides his time between Quito, Ecuador and Reykjavík, Iceland.

Diego Lama was born in Naples and is an architect. He has won several literary prizes in Italy, including the 2015 Premio Tedeschi for his novel La collera di Napoli (Giallo Mondadori) and the 2015 Premio Gran Giallo Città di Cattolica for his short story "Tre cose" (Giallo Mondadori).

Jace Lee (이주은) is a painter and poet born in Seoul and based in Cleveland, Ohio. Her practice is based on observation, play, and order, drawing from imagery and themes found in her dreams and everyday experiences.

Kurt Luchs is the author of *Falling in the Direction of Up* (SM, 2020), *One of These Things Is Not Like the Other* (Finishing Line Press, 2019), and *It's Funny Until Someone Loses an Eye (Then It's Really Funny)* (SM, 2017). He lives in Michigan.

Melissa McCarthy transmits from a tracking station in Edinburgh, Scotland. She's written *Photo, Phyto, Proto, Nitro* (SM, 2023) and *Sharks, Death, Surfers: An Illustrated Companion* (Sternberg, 2019). She's fond of Melville. See sharksillustrated.org for more.

Kat Meads's most recent book is *These Particular Women* (SM, 2023).

Matt Morris is the author of *Nearing Narcoma*, selected by Joy Harjo as winner of the Main Street Rag Poetry Award, and *Walking in Chicago with a Suitcase in My Hand* (Knut House Press). His poems have appeared in various magazines and anthologies, for which he has received multiple award nominations, including the Pushcart Prize and Best of the Net. He was recently named chief editor of *Home Planet News*.

Kirsten Mosher is a visual artist and writer living in Massachusetts. Her flash-book, *Zero (minutes to) Home*, was published by Selektion (Frankfurt, 2021), and her chapbook, *Plea$e Steal Me for 100 Plus Dollar-zz*, has been recently published by Lily Poetry Review Books. She's published in *Ellipsis Zine*, the *Bath Flash Fiction Anthology*, *The Cormorant Broadsheet*, *Sonder Magazine*, and is forthcoming in *Minor Literature[s]*. Her series Automotive Stories occasionally show up in the Automotive sections of local newspapers. She's currently working toward an exhibit at Frac Pays de La Loire in Carquefou, Nantes, France, opening November 2024.

M.J. Nicholls is the author of the novels *Trimming England* (SM, 2021), *Scotland Before the Bomb* (SM, 2019), The *1002nd Book to Read Before You Die* (SM, 2018), *The Quiddity of Delusion* (SM, 2017), *The House of Writers* (SM, 2016), and *A Postmodern Belch* (2014). He lives in Glasgow.

David Ossman has been a poet all his life, but is best known for being one-fourth of the Firesign Theatre, a comedy group that created and performed radio plays, record albums and stage productions starting in the 1960s and up into the new millennium. In addition, he is the author of two mystery novels, two memoirs and a huge body of work in audio theater for radio, CDs and stage.

Patrick Parks is author of a novel, *Tucumcari*, and has had fiction, poetry, reviews and interviews appear or forthcoming in a number of places, most recently *The Writing Disorder, TYPO, Change Seven*, and *Ocotillo Review*. He is a graduate of the University of Iowa's Writers' Workshop and lives with his wife near Chicago.

Geoffrey Pitcher grew up in the Greater Boston area, then taught American Studies at the University of Poitiers, France, for many years. Currently, he lives in southwestern France, where he gardens and cooks, lingers in spots of time, and tends to the contemplative life. When the weather is anything more promising than abysmal, he can be found at the shore, clamming and exploring.

Andrew Reichard is an author who lives in Grand Rapids, Michigan. His short fiction has appeared in journals such as *The Collagist, Black Static, Into the Void, decomP*, and others.

Cliff Saunders is the author of several poetry chapbooks, including *Mapping the Asphalt Meadows* (Slipstream Publications) and *The Persistence of Desire* (Kindred Spirit Press). His poems have appeared recently in *I-70 Review, Orchards Poetry Journal, Hidden Peak Review, Cacti Fur*, and *The Heartland Review*.

Kathrine Savu has been a professional artist for fifty years. Based in northern Michigan, her work often reflects regional cultural themes, yet occasionally diverges into global commentary and the experimental. Her primary medium is acrylic on canvas, though also recognized and commissioned for large murals installed throughout Michigan.

Mike Silverton's poetry appeared in the late 60s and early 70s in *Harper's, The Nation, Wormwood Review, Poetry Now, some/thing, Chelsea, Prairie Schooner, Elephant* and elsewhere. William Cole included Mike's poems in four anthologies: *Eight Lines and Under* (Macmillan, 1967), *Pith and Vinegar* (Simon and Schuster, 1969), *Poetry Brief* (Macmillan, 1971), and *Poems One Line & Longer* (Grossman, 1973).

Aug Stone is author of *Sporting Moustaches* (SM, 2024) the comedy novels *The Ballad Of Buttery Cake Ass* and *Off-License To Kill*, and the memoir *Nick Cave's Bar*. His journalism has appeared in *The Quietus, The Comics Journal, Under The Radar*, and many more sites and magazines. Aug was a founding member of H Bird and The Soft Close-Ups, and has played in countless other bands. He performs comedy as absurdist stream-of-consciousness raconteur, Young Southpaw.

Angela Townsend is Development Director at Tabby's Place: a Cat Sanctuary. She has an M.Div. from Princeton Theological Seminary and B.A. from Vassar College. Her work has appeared or will be published in upcoming issues of *The Amethyst Review, Braided Way, Dappled Things, Fathom Magazine*, and *Young Ravens Literary Review*, among others.

Thomas Walton is the author of *Good Morning Bone Crusher!* (Spuyten Duyvil 2021), *All the Useless Things Are Mine* (SM, 2020), *The World Is All That Does Befall Us* (Ravenna Press, 2019), and, with Elizabeth Cooperman, *The Last Mosaic* (SM, 2018). He works as an assistant clerk in the Department of Hairy Affairs in Tubdrain's West Coast offices.

Henry Wessells is author of *Another green world* (2003), *The Private Life of Books* (2014; new ed., 2020), and *A Conversation larger than the Universe* (2018).

David Wolf is the author of six collections of poetry, *Open Season, The Moment Forever, Sablier I, Sablier II, Visions* (with artist David Richmond), and *Weir* (a micro-chapbook from Origami Poems Project). His work has appeared in numerous literary magazines and journals, including *BlazeVOX, Cleaver Magazine, dadakuku, decomp, E·ratio, Indefinite Space, Lotus-eater Magazine, New York Quarterly, Otoliths*, and *River Styx Magazine*. He is a professor emeritus of English at Simpson College and serves as the poetry editor for *Janus Head: Journal of Interdisciplinary Studies in Literature, Continental Philosophy, Phenomenological Psychology, and the Arts*.

Don Zancanella has won the John S. Simmons/Iowa Short Fiction Award and an O.Henry Prize. He is the author of two novels, *Concord* (Serving House Books) and *A Storm in the Stars* (Delphinium/HarperCollins). A third one, *Animals of the Alpine Front*, will be out in 2024.

www.ingramcontent.com/pod-product-compliance
Lightning Source LLC
Chambersburg PA
CBHW081326020726
47506CB00006B/1196